Effects of Resettlement Schemes on the Biophysical and Human Environments:

The Case of the Gambela Region, Ethiopia

Andy Golda's Book andrewgolda@yahoo.com

Mengistu Woube

Universal Publishers
Boca Raton, Florida
USA • 2005

Effects of Resettlement Schemes on the Biophysical and Human Environments:
The Case of the Gambela Region, Ethiopia

Front Cover: Resettlement village with Cordia abyssinica R.Br (Boraginaccae) in Central Gambela.

Photos: Except Figure 29, all photos in this book were taken by the author.

Universal Publishers
Boca Raton, Florida • USA
2005

ISBN: 1-58112- 483-X

www.universal-publishers.com

**To the memory of my father, Woube Mengesha and
My mother, Mantegbosh Gubena**

TABLE OF CONTENTS

LIST OF FIGURES

LIST OF TABLES

1 ACKNOWLEDGEMENTS

I wish to express my heartfelt thanks to my dear wife, Woizero Almaz Kebede, without whose assistance, understanding and encouragement, I would not have been able to complete this book. I also wish to express my gratitude other members of my family: Ato Jemberu Dessalegn, Woizero Birtukan Endale, Yetnayet, Abyu and Kirubel Jemberu who supported me in many ways. Through Prof. Darge Wole, two other anonymous referees read the final manuscript and offered detailed criticisms and useful suggestions, which helped me to make more substantial improvements. I am extremely grateful to all of them. Some of the sections in Chapters 4, 8, 10 and 12 were adapted from my own published articles with kind permission from the following publishers: Northeast African Studies, Elsevier Science Ltd., John Wiley and Sons Ltd. and Malaria Research Centre in India for which I am grateful. Some of this work was written when I had a Visiting Research Position at the African Study Centre and the Department of Geography, Michigan State University, USA. I therefore would like to thank all the staff particularly Prof. David Wiley, Prof. Assefa Mehretu and Dr. Yacob Fisseha for their kind administrative support and friendship. As a Visiting Research Fellow at the Department of Geography and Associate Researcher at the Institute of Development Research, Addis Ababa University, I enjoyed their friendly co-operation and encouragement from all the staff for which I am thankful to all and Prof. Mekete Belachew in particular for the critical comments and suggestions on the earlier version and Dr. Beyene Doilicho for his administrative skills. I wish to express my thanks to the staff of the National Herbarium at the Addis Ababa University and the National Soil Service Project in Ethiopia for their laboratory assistance. And also thanks to Ato Lealem Birhanu who allowed me to use his photo cited in Figure 29. I owe special thanks to Ms Sue Edwards for language checking. I am indebted to Associate Prof. Abdulaziz Lodhi and Edward Ledwaba for their continuous encouragement and technical support. I also thank Dr. Beyene Petros and Prof. Afework Bekele for their constructive criticisms on earlier versions on malaria and wildlife Chapters respectively. Finally, I thank to Håkan Selin, David Gloriam and Tahir Mazloomian for their technical support.

While all the above and many others have contributed immeasurably, I alone am responsible for the views and conclusions presented in this book.

Mengistu Woube
Afro-Scandinavian Service (ASS)
March 2005.

CHAPTER 1: INTRODUCTION

1.1 The Issues

The main theme of the study, on which this book is based, is a comprehensive assessment of the effect of the traditional settlement patterns and resettlement schemes on the biophysical and human environments in Ethiopia in general, with special emphasis on the Gambela Region, south-western Ethiopia. The book initially dwells on the effects of settlement and resettlement processes in Africa and in other countries together with resettlement theory processes and typologies. Thereafter, the concern is the characteristics of the settlements and resettlement processes in the Gambela Region, which is the area of Ethiopia that has been exposed to large-scale resettlement schemes. This is accompanied by discussions on the overall impact of the settlement and resettlement processes on biophysical and human environments.

What follows is an analysis of the effects of the resettlements on the natural resources of soil, water and vegetation, land use and the farming systems in the area, and health conditions in the pre-and post resettlement Gambela. The impacts of fires on the plant communities and soils, as well as wars and settlement changes on the wildlife and their natural habitats are also discussed.

The main findings of this work are the following:
Most of the resettlement projects were designed with only short-sighted political gains in mind. Hence, they have operated as isolated entities, rather than as integrated development programmes. This has led to land-use and ethnic conflicts, deforestation, and land degradation, damaging floods, food shortages and outbreaks of various diseases. Such environmentally damaging experiences resulting from misconceived and misdirected policies should provide important lessons to those countries that wish to embark up on workable resettlement schemes or programmes.

It is unfortunate that Ethiopia has not succeeded in introducing sustainable rehabilitation schemes. The ones launched since the 1950s have ended up in population displacement, disruption of local agrarian and biophysical structures, and overall human and environment crises. The ethnic-based regional policy and the structural adjustment programme have aggravated these crises. The findings from the Gambela Region case study show that the 1980s Resettlement Schemes ignored the recommendations provided by experts as well as the indigenous people's time-and-experience-tested traditional knowledge regarding the value and conservation of the natural resources. With appropriate planning, alternative land-use and resettlement systems and conservation measures could have been adopted and implemented.

1.2 The Objectives

The specific objectives of this investigation are to: (a) examine settlement theories, processes and typologies; (b) describe the characteristics of the settlements and resettlements in the Gambela Region; (c) point out the effects of the settlement and resettlement processes on the overall biophysical and human environments in Ethiopia; (d) examine the effects of the resettlement schemes on the natural resources, land use, and farming systems; (e) discuss the effects of fires on the plant communities and soils; (f) indicate the effects of fires, wars and settlement changes on the wildlife and their natural habitats along the Baro-Akobo (Gambela) and Pibor-Sobat (Sudan) River Basins; (g) and to investigate the effects of the resettlement schemes on the health of the population with emphasis on the spatial spread of malaria in pre- and post-resettlement Gambela.

1.3 Methodology and Data Sources

The main methodology used is qualitative, i.e. observations and descriptions of the various phenomena or themes treated in the study. But where appropriate statistical or quantitative techniques, Geographic Information System (GIS) and other cartographic methods have been used. Generally, secondary data have been used to discuss global settlement and resettlement patterns and processes. Many of these have been obtained through visits to resettlement sites in Israel, South Africa, India, Tanzania, Kenya etc. The data on the Ethiopian settlements and resettlement schemes are mostly primary being original collected by the author through field surveys and observations carried out in the northern, southern, south-western and eastern parts of the country. The data on the Gambela Region were made available through extended field surveys and observations carried out in repeated visits.

To be able to determine the soil nutrient status of the post-resettlement periods, 35 soil samples were collected in 1991 from the five land-use types (forest, grass, traditional settlement and farmland, resettlement and a mechanised farm) in the Abobo District. The pH was measured in a 1:1 soil: H_2O ratio using standard glass and calomel electrodes. Available phosphorous (P) was determined by the Bray II method (Bray & Kurtz, 1945) and organic carbon was determined by the Walkley and Black (1935) method. The percentage of organic matter was calculated by multiplying the Walkley-carbon value by a factor of 1.724. Total Nitrogen (N) was determined by the macro Kjeldhal procedure as described by Wang (1986). The K and Cation Exchange Capacity (CEC) were determined by ammonium acetate extraction, magnesium (Mg) by atomic absorption, and sodium (Na) and calcium (Ca) by flame emission spectroscopy. Texture was identified in the field by physical observation and also determined in the laboratory by the pipette method.

In order to understand whether the post-resettlement floods were caused by high amounts of rainfall or by resettlement (land-use) activities, the 1977–1989 Alwero River discharge data at Abobo, calculated from the catchment area of 2790 km^2, were used. Since some data from the Alwero River were missing or incomplete, the mean was taken from the deviation of the Gilo River discharge, which was complete. The statistical analytic method developed by the Land Water Development Project (1986) was used to derive the missing information. The following statistical formula was used:

$$a = \frac{\sum (x-x^1)(y-y^1)^2}{\sum (x-x^1)^2}$$

$$b = y-ax$$

Where:

x is the dicharge of Gilo River (m^3-y-^{1});

x^1 is the mean discharge of Gilo River;

y is the discharge of Alwero river (m^3 y-^{1});

y^1 is the mean discharge of Alwero river and

a and b are constants, giving the result
$y = 0.1076x - 0.0185$

As far as vegetation was concerned the physiognomy of the plants, and forest management in the traditional settlement and the resettlement areas were studied. In order to understand the post-resettlement environmental changes concerning the degradation of vegetation and land, XS-SPOT images (band 1, scene 229/334 and band 2, scene 230/334, December 1986 and see also Figure 22) and topographic maps (scale 1:50000, 1982) were used. The types of techniques and methods are mentioned below.

In order to understand the effects of the resettlement schemes on the forest resources, 23 plant species were selected that the indigenous people and the author classified as the most indispensable ones in the region. In the field, an attempt was also made to understand whether these plants were unique for the Gambela region, the cultural attachments and advantages of these plants for the people and the environment, how they had been treated before and why they were threatened after the resettlement schemes, and what measures should be taken to save these plants. The method for doing this included estimating the biomass (leaves, fruits, flowers, roots and bark) and the height and surface cover of the selected species. Samples for identification were put in press in numbered folded sheets of newspaper and taken to the National Herbarium, Addis Ababa University, for identification. Voucher specimens of the species have been preserved at the National Herbarium.

Regarding the impact of fires, data were obtained through close observation of the different seasons throughout the study period. These observations were coupled with discussions with the local people and development workers in the Region. As far as the impact of resettlements, fires and war on wildlife and their natural habitats were concerned, the data were obtained through observation of the various ecological zones in the different seasons, as well as discussions with the local people and development workers. The data concerning malaria were collected through observation and discussions with the settlers from the different resettlement sites and from the health stations as well as the Gambela Hospital.

Various cartographic, including pantographic techniques and statistical methods were used using the programmes EXCEL, POWER DRAW and GIS for statistical analysis, computer-based mapping and to carry out digital processing and image analyses of the SPOT data.

The socio-economic data were derived from discussions with the local people and their officials and from various documents.

An attempt has been made to examine the effects of resettlement using a large number of parameters that have been discussed rather extensively. Even after having done this, one cannot claim absolute satisfaction, as there are still other factors that have not been touched on. Among these are the religious and ethnic dimensions.

1.4 Significance of the Study

The results of the study can contribute meaningfully to the following areas of concern: the debate on the effects of settlements and resettlement schemes on the biophysical and human environments; the provision of supplementary teaching and reference materials in environmental and agricultural geography; the production of a theoretical model that represents, more accurately, the sequences of cause and effect in settlement and resettlement schemes or programmes, in particular in the study area, in order to provide planners and policy makers with important lessons for solving the problems associated with settlement and resettlement programs.

1.5 Organisation of the Book

The book commences with this introduction that covers the aims of the study, its objectives, methodology, and data sources and significance.

Chapters 2 and 3 deal with the development of a proposed analytical model, as well as theories, processes and typologies of settlement and resettlement processes in Africa.

Chapter 4 discusses the effects of the past settlement and resettlement processes on the overall biophysical and human environments in Ethiopia. The present resettlement programme is also briefly outlined.

Chapter 5 deals with the characteristics of the settlements and resettlements in the Gambela Region.

Chapters 6 and 7 cover the effects of the resettlements on the soil resources, land-use and farming systems.

Chapters 8, 9 and 10 and 11 include the effects of resettlement schemes on water, vegetation and plant communities in pre-and post-resettlement Gambela; and the effects of fires, wars and settlement on the wildlife and their natural habitats in the Baro-Akobo (Gambela) and Pibor-Sobat (Sudan) River Basins.

Further, the effects of resettlement on health with emphasis on the spatial spread of malaria are discussed in **Chapter 12**.

Finally, appendices, concluding remarks and references are presented.

2 CHAPTER 2: A PROPOSED ANALYTICAL MODEL FOR SETTLEMENT AND RESETTLEMENT PROCESSES IN AFRICA

2.1 The Spatio-Environmental Approach

An understanding of the spatio-environmental approach helps to explain, in part, how the spatial and biophysical environment, political and socio-economic factors, cultural and administrative systems affect the spatial distribution of settlement and resettlement patterns.

People have moved into and out of (re)settlement sites either by their own free will or because of exogenous factors. Over time humanity has moved from its original settlements in eastern Africa to new ones throughout the world. Such spatial processes were gradual, irregular, spontaneous, voluntary, and involuntary. The physical and social distances were short or long depending mainly on the availability of local resources, including fertile soils, water supply points, crop and grazing land, firewood, markets, fishing places, building materials and employment opportunities.

Prior to and during the mercantilist, colonial, post-colonial and post-industrial periods, and voluntary and involuntary global resettlements had occurred. Many countries have also developed and implemented planned settlement schemes. However, most of these schemes have not succeeded in improving the basic necessities of life. Rather, they had led to increase human suffering and environmental degradation (Chambers 1969, Schudder 1981, Hansen & Oliver-Smith, 1982).

Ironically, however, a number of governments in developing countries are still introducing settlement and resettlement schemes. One reason for this is that resettlement schemes are relatively easier to launch than, for example, agricultural reform programmes, introduction of new agricultural technologies, and the development of rural towns with conservation of natural resources. Various resettlement schemes have led to the concentration and intensification of human activities in environmentally sensitive areas like frontier and coastal ecosystems (Moran, 1989: 69-81).

In view of the gravity of environmental degradation problems world-wide, it is appropriate to examine their root causes and effects on soil, water, biodiversity, spatial spread of new diseases and the decline of agricultural productivity. Many studies have already been conducted including: the World Commission on Environment and Development (1987), the Earth Summit in Rio de Janeiro (UNs, 1992) and that on Human Settlement in Istanbul (HABITAT, 1996). Over 1998-1999, there were major fires in Asia and Greece, floods in China and USA, and devastating hurricane-related landslides in Honduras and Nicaragua. These are a few examples of the environmental disasters that are probably the result of human activities upsetting the climate of the world. Many studies advocate the adoption of sustainable approaches to balance the requirements of environmental stability and development to mitigate the problem of environmental degradation. According to Upreti (1994: 21), Sustainable Environmental Development "is the management and conservation of the natural resource base and the orientation of technological and institutional changes in such a manner as to ensure the attainment and continued satisfaction of human needs for present and future generations". Unfortunately, however, the problem of environmental degradation has remained unchanged or has worsened.

Hitherto, most research findings have indicated that resettlement schemes have not alleviated land use problems, nor have they transformed traditional subsistence economies into modern economies. In fact, the settlement patterns in many countries of the developing world, particularly those in Africa, have brought about negative changes in both the biophysical environment, such as land-degradation, and in the human environment leading to the social disorganisation of indigenous people.

Through the spatio-environmental approach, the push and pull factors of the resettlement processes can be better understood. For instance, factors that once pulled people from other areas can be treated as push factors at other times. This means that when the factors that attracted people to resettle are no longer able to provide for their basic well being due to environmental degradation, the settlers can be forced to move either back to their original settlements or elsewhere. Land-use right can be one of the push or pull factors. For instance, during the resettlement process the introduction of a new land-holding system will inevitably result in a change of land-use patterns, which, in turn, will affect the forms and types of settlement patterns. Changes in settlement patterns, introduction of new rural and urban institutions, and physical and social infrastructures (e.g. dams and roads) also contribute significantly to changes in the lifestyles of people. Changes in the government system can also bring about alterations to the existing relationship between people and the way they exploit their natural resources. Such readjustments or modifications lead to the restructuring of settlement sites, with changes in technology, crop specialisation and the conversion of grazing and forest land into cropland, or vice versa. The conversion of a natural landscape into a cultural landscape and the conversion of agricultural land into urban settlement have become common in many parts of the world.

The spatio-environmental approach is vital to understand human adaptation to natural hazards (such as floods, diseases and drought), changing patterns of land-use, and human and animal movements in any landscape along with the various push and pull factors. Ritter began the spatial study of settlements in the early 19th century. Since then, French and German geographers have developed this branch of geography (Baker, 1963). This approach gained emphasis in the literature during the 1960s (Bylund, 1960; Hägerstrand, 1965; Gould, 1969; Christaller, 1966, Hudson, 1969). However, from the 1970s onwards, only limited studies have been undertaken, mostly by sociologists, for example in Asia (Farmer, 1974 and HABITAT, 1986), in Africa (Prothero, 1976, and Stone, 1965), in Latin America (HABITAT, 1986, and Palmer, 1974). Such studies focused on spontaneous resettlements and gave little attention to the issues of planned settlements and resettlements.

Most geographic research and teaching endeavours in industrialised countries now focus on issues related to industrial-urban relations and technological changes. Geographers do not pay special attention to the issues of rural-urban interaction, landscape conversion, land-use and settlement changes, and biophysical and human environmental relationships. Undoubtedly, geography, as a discipline that straddles the natural and social sciences, can ask more relevant questions than other disciplines regarding the relationships of settlement and environment. Among such questions are: Where are settlement activities occurring? How will they affect the natural resources and human lives? How can the biodiversity and natural habitats be sustained and managed for future generations in the face of changes in settlement patterns?

The resettlement schemes in most African and Asian countries take place in marginal areas, most of which are prone to disasters like drought, flood and diseases. Use of the spatio-environmental approach would help to describe the biophysical and human environmental systems, man-land relationships and the spatial distribution of populations. As Hudson (1976) argues, the study of (re)settlement processes ought to be viewed in association with certain spatial factors such as climate, topography and access to infrastructure in order to indicate the locations for and accessibility to the resettlement sites, land-use changes and other factors affecting settlement patterns. Well-planned (re)settlements will help considerably to mitigate environmental deterioration.

Gol'ts (1986) contends that the study of (re)settlement processes is one branch of geography, since the (re)settlement areas and their territorial linkages reflect a great diversity of factors of a social, economic, demographic and biophysical character. The absence of integrated work plans among researchers, planners and policy-makers creates major obstacles to the improvement of (re)settlement sites. It is the geographers' duty to devise strategies for the management and conservation of the natural resources and ecosystems to benefit the human as well as all the other biotic communities. Geographers have developed special skills in using Geographic Information Systems (GIS) for the processing and analysing of data. Geographers can also contribute by using the Environmental Impact Assessment (EIA) tool for examining the interactions among biophysical, economic and socio-cultural impacts.

In order to achieve environmentally sustainable (re)settlement projects it is appropriate to comprehend the physical attributes, rural-urban interactions, land ownership and agricultural systems, and the local institutions of the areas under consideration. In short, geographers play a key role in addressing how (re)settlements interact with the biophysical environment in time and space in any region of the world.

Through environmentally sound and economically viable town planning for physical and social infrastructures, effective trade links and communications can be provided. Such measures encourage people to invest in the more labour-intensive light industries and allow migrant workers to move from rural to urban areas. These measures can also lead to the development of appropriate technologies and contribute to the conservation of natural resources.

At this juncture it would be appropriate to grasp clearly the concept of environment. It denotes the whole biotic (living) community in a given area together with its abiotic (non-living) components forming an interacting system through which energy flows and nutrients circulate to create the ecosystem of the area (Strange, 1980). The dynamic interaction between the biotic and abiotic elements creates the distinction between the biophysical and cultural landscape. For the purpose of this study the term environment is defined as the surrounding condition characterised by the interplay between the biophysical and human characteristics of an area.

Figure 1 is the conceptual model, which has been developed to indicate how the human and biophysical environments are related to the (re)settlement processes. In the Figure the first box represents the various elements of the human environment (demography, settlement morphology, land-use, cultural systems, health facilities and cultures) and the second box indicates the components of the biophysical environment (geomorphology, soils, topography, vegetation, climate and energy). The biophysical environment provides man with benefits of air, water, food and shelter, but it is also exposed to hazards like floods, drought, hunger, diseases and deaths. The biophysical environment can either be destroyed or improved by the activities of man. High population density, mobility, and poor housing conditions and inadequate food (Prothero, 1976), for example, can worsen health problems. They can also be improved through integrated development that mitigates the problems through local, regional and international co-operation. In short, unless balanced socio-economic systems are maintained the biophysical environment can have a negative impact on the human environment and vice-versa.

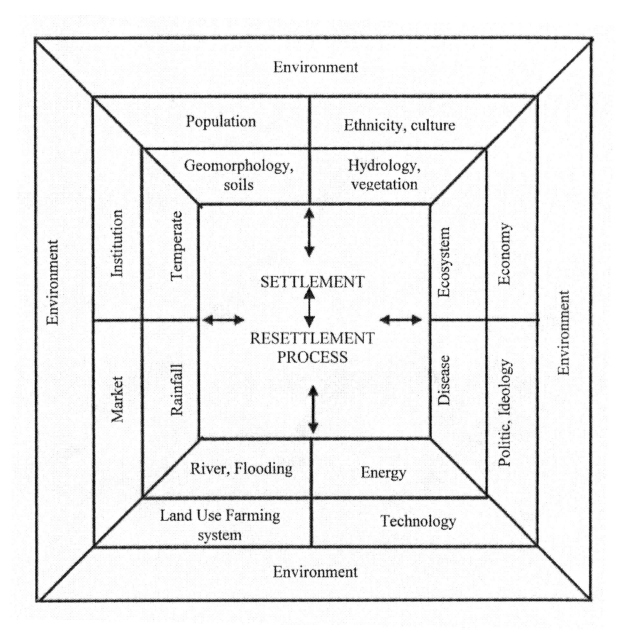

Figure 1. The conceptual model showing the relationship among the resettlement processes and the biophysical and human environments.

Unsustainable utilisation of natural resources often destroys local food resources. It also results in the rapid destruction of the biophysical and human landscapes, which further limits the spaces available for settlement by rural and urban dwellers. As poorly planned settlement and resettlement sites grow in time and space, the deterioration of the biophysical and human environments can not be confined within one landscape but spread out to the surrounding regions or areas.

3 CHAPTER 3: THE SETTLEMENT THEORIES, PROCESSES AND TYPOLOGIES

Settlement Geography has been variously defined and interpreted. It includes settlement units consisting of size, location, function and morphology; settlement groups, including settlement hierarchy, spacing and fields of influence; and settlement society comprising history, population and social cohesion (Whynne-Hammond, 1985). To Stone (1965: 355) "settlement is the description and analysis of the distribution of buildings by which people attach themselves to the land for the purposes of primary production". To Jordan (1966: 27), the above definition is narrow and unfitting to Settlement Geography. Instead, he defines the term as "the study of the form of the cultural landscape". Chisholm (1962:126) defines Settlement Geography as "the distribution and patterns of farms and farmsteads, as well as the population movement between and within the (re)settlement sites in the biophysical and cultural landscape". For the purpose of this study, *settlement* is defined as the original place where individuals or a group of people adapt themselves to the existing biophysical and social systems.

Resettlement is defined as the process by which individuals or a group of people leave spontaneously or unspontaneously their original settlement sites to resettle in new areas where they can begin new trends of life by adapting themselves to the biophysical, social and administrative systems of the new environment. Time is of the essence in (re)settlement processes. During the relocation and adaptation process, resettlers may face both physical and mental stress. The movements can either occur in the form of migration, refugee and mobility, or emergency and forced resettlement processes that are distinguished from resettlement schemes. Mobility can be divided into (a) spatial, which includes all sorts of movements and (b) social, which refers to a change in the socio-economic status of individuals or groups (Kosinski et al. (eds), 1975, and Wood, 1977). A person can migrate or become a refugee due to human-made or natural phenomena, and he can resettle himself or be resettled by others. This form of movement to resettlement sites is often unplanned, irregular, less permanent, cyclical in character and can either be short or long-distance movement (Wood, 1977). However, in some cases the new resettlement sites can be planned after the resettlers have arrived in the new sites.

Under spontaneous resettlement the resettlers may or may not break their ties with their original places. Such resettlement processes take place either by virtue of individual decisions or natural calamity, or due to the availability of economic resources. For example, the worsening of ecological conditions, land-use problems, land scarcity, ethnic conflicts and natural hazards in the original settlement can lead to the need for resettlement. In this respect the push factor can have a negative impact whereas the pull factor attracts people to resettle (Kosinski et al. (eds), 1975 and Prothero, 1976: 32). New ideas and better local economic resources often attract the resettlers.

A *resettlement scheme* may be defined as a planned project or programme involving the transfer of people most probably through selection and control from one region to another. When (re)settlement schemes are considered, governments in developing countries, in general, and in Africa, in particular, make decisions as to when, where and how reestablishment should take place. Private agencies or national or international organisations such as the World Bank can sponsor such schemes. Unlike the spontaneous resettlement process, movement in the resettlement schemes is brought about by government policy either through a voluntary or involuntary process.

Four main resettlement theories will be discussed: These include morphology, location, diffusion and ecological distribution.

3.1 Morphology and Location

According to Mukherji (1976), three basic elements help explain morphological changes in the (re)settlement process namely: type, form or shape, and patterns. *Type* explains the formal and functional relationship of the resettlement site, i.e. house-to-house, house-to-street and street-to-street relationships. The type of houses and farms are included in this category. *Form* refers to the geometrical shape of the aggregate of buildings and streets. The *shapes* of farms, buildings and streets such as square, circular or rectangular are explicitly indicated. A settlement form can be described as scattered or dispersed in which families form a village or urban community.

In geography, settlement forms refer to the distribution of individual huts, which can be dispersed or clustered. A dispersed settlement is defined as a dwelling situated in the farm site and owned by an individual. A clustered or nucleated settlement is characterised by compact groupings of huts or houses outside the farming area. Farmers are able to design a dispersed settlement through understanding the microenvironment that includes the fertility of the soil and moisture supply, health advantages and physical distance (Chisholm, 1979). With respect to the physical and cultural landscape there is another form of settlement, namely in a row or linear. Settlements can be located along a flood plain, or along roads or railways. Huts are usually formed by a nuclear family. When population increases in size, villages can create clustered settlements known as neighbourhoods. The number of huts can vary from 20 to more than 30. This type of settlement can be formed through kinship affiliation and mutual responsibility.

Pattern describes the geometrical arrangement of a large number of urban and rural settlements that fit into natural and cultural features to determine whether a pattern is clustered, dispersed, linear, in a row, and random, and to what degree of each. Morphological change can also be explained by land-use changes which in turn lead to social and political conflicts, strengthening or weakening of rural institutions and deterioration of the ecological systems. On the other hand, a marginal landscape can be converted into mosaic and beautiful cultural landscape.

Although early geographers contributed significantly to the subject of settlement, Christaller's (1966) contribution was considerable. The Central Place Theory, which Christaller built up, rests on the hypothesis that a certain amount of productive land must support each urban centre, and that the centre exists where it does in order to perform essential services for the surrounding region. Trade is the first of these services. Other services include banking, handicraft industries, state administration, cultural and spiritual offerings (churches, schools, and museums), professional and business organisations, transportation and sanitation.

It is not actually the place or settlement that is central. The concept of centrality refers to the central function being performed by the place. Christaller compares central places with dwellings where settlers live and depend upon agricultural activities, mining, industrial and social services. A settlement site in itself can be considered as a central place if this site provides public services to the neighbouring villages or towns. Christallers approach of settlement hierarchies is useful to the understanding of the structure, functions, and patterns of settlement schemes and the distance of the central place from which all the individuals living in an area can acquire goods and services and other types of local economic resources. Distance plays a role in the spatial distribution of population, use of basic economic resources, settlements and the likes. Christaller expresses geographical-distance in terms of economics or cost-distance including such factors as time spent and freight costs. Like Christaller, Lösch (1954) considered distance between the market area and the settlement sites. As one goes from the central market to a given distance the price of goods becomes relatively higher and the demand for some expensive goods becomes lower.

To Chisholm (1979) a geographical distance equals human time – the cost in time converted into monetary terms. Chisholm based his studies on costs incurred in relation to geographical distance between the (re)settlement sites and the resource bases in the countries of Italy, Spain, Finland and the Netherlands, and attempted to convert physical distance to the time it takes a person to cover a given distance.

Some classical economists, for example Ricardo (1953) and Von Thünen (1966), are known for their theory of Economic Rent and its application to the study of (re)settlement schemes. Economic Rent is not used to explain the relationship between land and land rent, but rather to show the various costs, which include the physical distances between agricultural settlement and human (re)settlement sites and central market places. Although these economists differ from each other in their approaches they arrived at a final conclusion giving the same connotation regarding physical distance and settlement sites. For Ricardo the gain attained from land (e.g. economic rent) is dependent on the fertility of the soil. The process of expansion taking place in and around the central market places and settlement sites affects the degree of demand shown for crops. This demand can be appreciably increased by the cultivation of fertile land. However, since such land often belongs to a few people, the demand becomes high and the increased economic rent benefits only the few. Consequently, the shortage of fertile land creates higher land rent and thus forces many people to resettle on infertile land. Even though land-use rights and land rent are given similar treatment concerning fertile and infertile land, agricultural inputs for the infertile land are less than for the fertile land.

Von Thünen took Ricardo's Economic Rent concept and adapted it to his location theory regarding the transport of agricultural products in Northern Germany. He relates Economic Rent to the problems caused by distance and computed Economic Rent in relation to distance from the central settlement. Von Thünen argues that the economic advantage of the land is dependent upon its distance from the central market or central settlement. In other words, the closer the land is to the market centre the higher its productivity and the socio-economic services also become better.

The differences and similarities of the two approaches can be summarised as follows: for Ricardo the Economic Rent is mainly dependent on the fertility of the land. Hence, the further one goes away from the central settlement the poorer becomes the fertility of the land and the lower the Economic Rent.

According to Von Thünen, however, land is assumed to be homogeneous. What concerned him most was the distance from the central market place and the subsequent transport costs. It is not the fertility of land that matters but the various economic advantages gained, due to the proximity of the land to the central market place. Hence, the shorter the distance from a central market place the higher is the economic rent and vice-versa. Both Ricardo and Von Thünen were concerned about the viability of land and the new settlement site in terms of monetary values. Socio-psychological values were not considered in their studies of settlements. They argued that a longer distance from the central market place results in higher the production costs, with lower prices for the produce so that the land becomes relatively poorer in quality and receives little inputs with increasing distance from the central market. Many recent writers in the West reject the theory of Economic Rent as having no application in the modern world. But Chisholm (1962) argued that it is not the particular findings that count but their methods of analyses, which may be applied to any situation at any time or place.

This author believes that it is important to understand Ricardo's argument regarding the fertility of the land in relation to the (re)settlement processes. This is because since land is associated closely with the political system and socio-economic growth or decline of certain agrarian countries, those who have economic and political power control it. Von Thünen's theory appears to have relevance for most of the developing countries. For example Horvath (1969) studied some of the location and settlement patterns and problems of Ethiopia focusing on the principal urban market of Addis Ababa and the impact of geographical distance on the supply of marketable agricultural produce to urban settlements. Edward (1977) identified remarkable parallels between the agricultural settlement patterns of colonial Mexico during the period of Spanish rule and Von Thünen's land-use theory. Bylund (1960) and Norling (1960) were of the opinion that it is important to measure the geographical-distance (e.g. the time taken to arrive at a given central settlement place) and the evolution of (re)resettlement around it. Dacey (1962) focused on the techniques of nearest-neighbour analysis and their application to the measurement of the geographical-distance between the central settlement places and the peripheral settlements. Assefa (1986) studied the spatial problems related to the distribution of production in Africa. This study provided a good time/space model, which focused on the problems of the distribution of supply from and between the central settlements and the peripheral settlements.

There is also the problem of social distance in the (re)settlement schemes. The social distance problem is realised when the (re)settlers arrive and experience the early stages of adjustment. At that time the social distances between the different ethnic, income, status and professional groups begin to emerge. Moreover, some groups of people cannot afford the high costs of time and cash to travel and visit their families who reside in widely distributed (re) settlement sites. The social distance is created not only between and among resettlers but also between them and officials in the settlement areas and it can be worsened in poorly designed (re)settlement schemes. Such problems may force resettlers to abandon their (re)settlement sites and move to other ecological zones. The relocation and adaptation processes in any resettlement site will be discussed in Chapter 4.

3.2 The Diffusion and Ecological Distribution Theories

It is known that the diffusion theory is widely practised or applied in the natural sciences, particularly in plant and animal studies. It has also become an important concern for researchers in geography.

Geographers are interested in the diffusion or spread of phenomena over space and time. Therefore, for geographers it is spatial diffusion that is of particular interest to them. Hägerstrand (1965); Gould (1969) and Hudson (1972) attempted to interpret the diffusion theory as it applied to the location of (re)settlements. Their studies focused on the interaction, spread, contact, change and growth of (re)settlement patterns and the physical distances separating the original settlements from the new (re)settlements, the local economic resource sites and central settlement places.

Empirical investigations have identified three types of diffusion processes. The first type reveals that the first adapters or innovators, who are the early majority, are followed by the second adapters who are the late majority; and the third adapters are those who arrive last, i.e. the "laggards" (Brown et al., 1971 and Gould, 1969). The reasons why a new area or innovation is adapted rapidly or slowly have to do with the characteristics of geographical barriers such as mountains, rivers, lakes, deserts, languages, cultures, ethnicity, income and bureaucracy (Hägerstrand, 1965).

The second type is the spread of human settlers from the neighbouring places or centres. This phenomenon is divided into expansion and relocation diffusion. The former refers to the diffusion of central settlements and the latter refers to the phenomena that are being diffused. The third empirical regularity explains how the innovation starts first in the central settlement and then spreads to marginal (re)settlement sites. In sum, the linkages between the central settlement places affect the agglomerations of many individuals and peripheral settlements at the local, regional, national and international levels (Hägerstrand 1965 and Gould 1969).

The population movements of a certain area manifest four stages: (a) the first stage refers to the physical transfer of resettlers to the new settlement sites; (b) the adaptation process to the biophysical and human environments; (c) the achievement of socio-economic development by the resettlers; and (d) the resettlers are able to manage the biophysical and human environments. Hudson's "ecological distribution theory" explains the laws of spatial distribution by comparing the process of human settlements to the process of competition in plant ecology. To Hudson the (re)settlements process and plant adaptation in one area pass through three stages of development, namely: colonisation, spread and competition. The author, however, prefers the term occupation to colonisation since the latter term can provide an erroneous impression. But the term occupation explains that resettlers and plants want to adapt themselves to the new geographical territory or environment. The adaptation process involves the spread of settlers and plants in the newly occupied area. Competition connotes the fights over the available geographical space by the resettlers or newcomers.

According to Haining (1982), Hudson's theory provides a complete spatial theory of the resettlement process. He has given more attention to the "spatial derivatives" of the process rather than to the socio-economic and psychological factors. On the other hand Grossman (1971) argued that Hudson's biologically derived principles do not apply to human settlement patterns which are often centrally planned rather than being arranged randomly. But even Grossman himself believes that Hudson's hypothesis has some importance since it applies to a given (re)settlement pattern. Hudson admits that although the non-spatial aspects of ecological theories are quiet unlike the settlement theories the spatial properties are similar. This author argues that the plant species must have places of origin and agents of movement. Plants can be introduced into new areas through biological and human agents. People who are required to move and resettle in new areas do so by government directives. Such movements take place in three stages: (a) government considers (re)settlement areas and selects people for resettlement; (b) resettlers are moved to re-establish settlement sites; and (c) resettlers require some time to adapt to the new environment. Hudson's approach, however, is less applicable to the government-sponsored resettlement schemes. As he himself admits this is because the ecological distribution theory is not appropriate for the planned resettlements. The settlement distribution and adaptation processes can further be explained through biological evolution of (re)settlements. Before we do that the type of settlements has to be identified.

3.3 The Resettlement Processes and Typologies of Resettlements

Four types of resettlement schemes can be identified in a given country, namely: spontaneous, emergency and forced, voluntary, and involuntary. These may be grouped into non-planned resettlements including spontaneous and emergency, and forced resettlements and planned settlements comprising voluntary and involuntary resettlements. These typologies are presented in Figure 2.

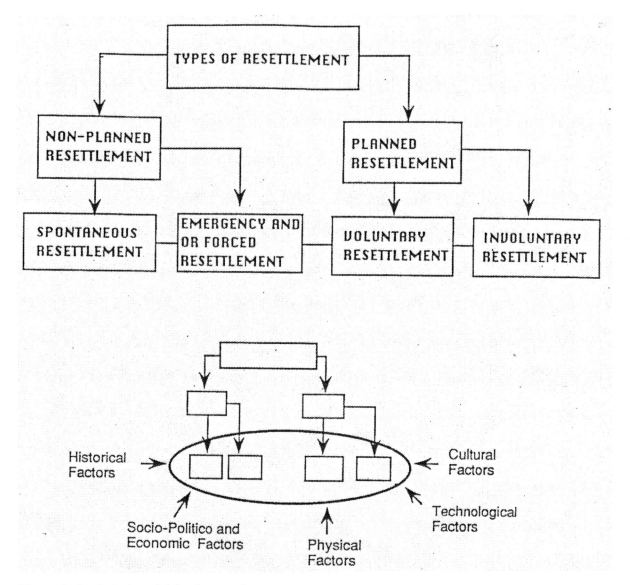

Figure 2. Analytical model for the resettlement processes

> **Note:** The processes fall within five explanatory frameworks. The causes for these processes include historical, ecological, natural calamity, and human factors.

3.4 The Non-Planned Resettlements

3.4.1 Spontaneous resettlement

The spontaneous resettlement process is often associated with agricultural resettlement in which farmers relocate themselves in response to external and internal influences in their original settlements.

The relocation process takes place either in already settled areas or areas that have never been settled before. The processes of such resettlement are not homogeneous in their patterns of development. Rather they manifest different origins and varieties of organisational forms and differing objectives and motivations. Such processes may lead to the increase of agricultural production or may also be associated with the destruction of natural resources. Among the many factors that affect the process of spontaneous resettlement the following are the major ones: historical, trading, and colonisation.

3.4.2 The historical evolution of settlements

African countries are believed to have similar historical factors that have influenced the settlement process. Paleo-environmental and paleo-anthropological and archaeological evidence indicates that humans in Africa originated from one 'African Eve' who lived in the Omo-Valley of Ethiopia, around Lake Turkana of Kenya and in the Olduvai-Gorge in Tanzania at least five million years ago. Ethiopia is known to be one of the earliest homes of mankind. The skeleton named "*Dinkinesh*"(which means wonderful in *Amharic* – Ethiopian language) was found in the Ethiopian Rift Valley. This was an important discovery as it confirmed that the human species originated in Eastern Africa. The earliest hominids moved from their original settlements to the northern, southern and western parts of Africa. As Tobias (1978) argued, it is Africa that cradled the infancy of mankind. Modern humanity emerged from Africa to conquer the earth and settle in the mountains, hills, plateaus, islands and valleys of the world. Recent genetic studies indicate that Adam was an African (Gibbons, 1997).

After many years the human race diffused from Africa to Eurasia and then to the Mediterranean of Europe, Australia, temperate Europe, north and South America and much later to the small Islands in and around the Pacific Ocean. For example, the Polynesians colonised Hawai and settled there about 400 years ago due to the shortage of arable land in their original settlements. They introduced new plants and animal species, built canals and dams, as well as introducing new farming and cropping systems in the new settlement sites.

Table 1 and Figure 3 show the time scale in millions of years of the human settlement processes from their original settlements in Africa to other parts of the globe. The global settlement processes took 28 different stages. These can be abridged to five main stages, namely: (a) initial stage of human settlement within Africa; (b) Africa-Asia divergence; (c) Asia-Australia divergence; (d) Europe-Asia divergence; and (e) Asia-America divergence. All these settlement processes took place alongside the processes of change in hominid body shape, biophysical-geographical changes, adaptation, curiosity and sense of destiny. In short, the early settlers were pushed and pulled by biogeographical factors. Through the settlement processes, new vegetation and animal species were met with and technological and cultural developments were developed in the settlement regions, which changed the physical landscape to the cultural ones. All these developments were later expanded through trade links between and across regions.

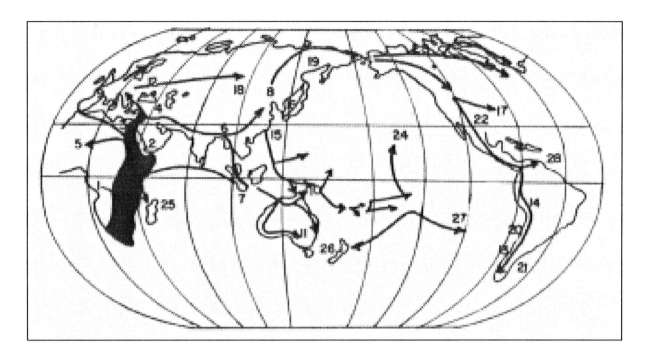

Figure 3. Areas of human origin and early settlement processes in twentyeight main stages

Table 1. Key to Figure 3

Stage	Year	Stage	Year
1	5.5 million	15	30 000
2	3.7 million	16	30 000
3	3 million	17	19 000
4	2 million	18	15 000
5	1.7 million	19	14 000
6	700 000	20	11-12 000
7	500 000	21	11-22 000
8	450 000	22	11 000
9	100 000	23	4 500
10	40 000	24	1 600
11	38 000	25	1 500
12	33 000	26	1 000
13	33 000	27	1 100
14	22 000	28	1 000

Source. National Geography, 1988 and Gamble, 1978.

3.4.3 Resettlement through trading

Prior to the disturbance by the Europeans of the original and regional trading systems, there were population movements and trade routes throughout Africa and between Africa and the other parts of the world. For example, an important trade route expanded from among the different countries of the Red Sea Basin along those of the Indian Ocean connection eventually the Far East and the Middle East. During the second millennium A.D., caravan trade routes were developed from Egypt to the territories of the Bogos and Beja pastoralists (in present-day Eritrea), the heart of the Ethiopian plateau and the coastal peoples in Somalia. These mutual benefit-trade relationships led to socio-political and economic developments, and perpetuated voluntary settlement processes within and across the Red Sea Basin (Abir, 1980). Through the Trans-Saharan trading system, and marine trade, since the late 15th century, the population in the Sahel region had indirect contact with the outside world (Grove, 1978).

Although the Afro-Asian trading systems continued to expand, these trading routes were disturbed through European expansion into North and South America followed by the slave trade, initiated by the Europeans. Four factors were responsible for pulling the Europeans into the New World: (a) warm coastlines; (b) accessibility by sea; (c) land suitability for cash crops; and (d) abundant labour through importing slaves from Africa. The warm climate provided the environment for rapid germination of seeds, plant growth and maturity of crops for trading. The sea was used to transport products and people from and to the original settlements. Although the slave trade peaked between 1700 and the early 1800s, European merchants had started it in the fifteenth century. In the same period, the European-merchants transported about 30 million African slaves to their colonies in North and South America and the West Indies (De Blij & Muller, 1988).

3.4.4 Resettlement through colonisation

The Europeans did not confine their activities to the slave trade only. The European representatives settled in Africa and then expanded their colonies. Among the leading figures that designed the colonial map of Africa were Cecil Rhodes for Britain, Karl Peters for Germany, and Pierre de Brazza for France, and Henry Stanley for the King of Belgium. Each colonial power chose a different general area to establish new settlements (De Blij et al., 1988). For instance, the Dutch chose the shores of South Africa as the site of permanent resettlement; the British settled in North America and the Indian sub-continent; the Spanish and Portuguese occupied South America; the British again moved to Australia and New Zealand, the French settled in New Caledonia, Morocco, Tunisia and Algeria; the Portuguese took Angola, Mozambique and Guinea Bissau, and the Italians occupied Libya, Eritrea and some parts of Somalia. The colonial powers settled spontaneously in their respective colonies without any restrictions (Gould, 1969, and Despois & Raynal, 1967).

The colonial governments forced the local people to abandon their original settlement sites. For example the British colonialists forced the inhabitants of the Ushi region in Northern Zimbabwe to abandon their original settlements and resettle in clustered sites (Kay, 1964). Apart from government supported colonialism, about 60 million Europeans settled in the different parts of North and South America, Southern Africa, Australia and New Zealand by pushing out the indigenous people. The settlers were pulled by the availability of economic resource sites such as unoccupied fertile land and woodlands (Jones, 1985). For example, thousands of people from the Scandinavian countries moved and settled in the valleys of the St. Croix and Mississippi Rivers in the USA between 1860 and 1900. After many generations the land tenure systems and population pressure in these regions brought about environmental stress. When the pull factors reached the stage of becoming the push factors, the settlers became aware of the possibility to settle elsewhere, and this involved the movement of their sons and daughters to resettle in the unexploited rich lands in South Dakota and Montana (Bodvall, 1959, 1988). The immediate causes of population movements to resettle in new regions of the USA were: (a) population increase in the small area of already settled arable land; (b) the winter of 1866 that was one of longest and hardest in memory; (c) lack of alternative employment opportunities outside agriculture; (d) agricultural production of low quality; and (e) lack of inter-regional communications networks (Bodvall, 1959; Mengistu, 1987 and Bylund, 1974).

3.4.5 Emergency and forced resettlement

Emergency and forced resettlement result from sudden or unexpected occurrences of hazardous situations, political measures, and group and individual decisions requiring the movements of people, or even of plants, from their original settlements to new ones. These settlements are interrelated and are caused by the following factors: natural calamities, population and environmental factors, human-induced factors and external factors.

3.4.6 Natural calamities

Natural calamities are earthquakes, volcanic eruptions, human and animal diseases (especially malaria, and trypanosomiasis), floods, drought, and famine. These can cause millions of people to leave their original settlements and resettle elsewhere (Prothero, 1976). The Bura ethnic group of Nigeria, for example, moved from the upland areas and resettled in the middle Hawal Valley in the beginning of the 1900s. Although the lowland region attracted people from the upland areas, out of the total of 52 resettled villages, 44 were deserted due to the outbreak of diseases (Bradley, 1974). In the Horn of Africa, civil war, drought and famine have displaced East Africa and the Sahelean regions millions of people. It was reported by the UNHCR, 1991) that Ethiopia hosted 367,800 refugee settlers in 1986. Out of these 276,000 came from Somalia, 73,000 from the Sudan, 18,000 from Djibouti and 8,000 from Kenya. The severe incidences of drought and floods are exacerbated by the prolonged exploitation of the natural resources. Such factors disrupt the social and biophysical environmental balance and aggravate the existing problems such as food shortage, regional conflicts and wars.

3.4.7 Population and environmental factors

High rates of population growth in small areas have created shortages of arable land, resulting in land-use and ethnic conflicts that can force people to abandon their original settlements in order to resettle elsewhere where employment opportunities exist. Such movements of people tend to be high in areas of environmental stress and in a country where there are no effective land reform programmes, rural industries and earnings from off-farm sources available. Large-scale, short and long-distance movements of labour within countries and across international boundaries are more common today than in the 1950s. In the 1970s an estimated 10 million workers moved from Northern Africa to the industrialised countries. Within Africa, between 1974 and 1980, more than 20 million people were resettled in other parts of Africa (Clark (1986).

The break down of relationships between individuals and groups, social ties or links with the original settlement places, high rates of population growth, lack of employment opportunities and social unrest can all lead to the resettlement of people. In 1988, for example, due to wars, more than 1 million people from El Salvador and Guatemala, up to 400,000 from Nicaragua, 2 million people from Iran and Iraq were forced to resettle within the respective countries and neighbouring regions. Both temporary and permanent resettlement occurs in the USA, Europe, Canada and Australia by people who migrate from the developing countries in the hope of finding an improved way of life (Leatherby, 1989 and Grove, 1989).

The concentration of human settlements in limited areas and environmentally unsound agricultural methods disturb the soil structure and texture in many parts of the developing world, particularly in Africa. Slash and burn cultivation techniques have been practised for thousands of years in many parts of the world. In recent years, however, farmers have begun to return to the areas that had been cleared and resettled previously, before the forests fully rehabilitate themselves. Under such circumstances soil erosion is likely to be aggravated. It was, and still is, one of the main causes of the decline of land productivity and crop yields which led to the downfall of civilisations in ancient Mesopotamia, the Middle East and in many parts of Africa (Troeh et al., 1980). Soil erosion was also one of the reasons for the collapse of the Mayan civilisation. The Brazilian civilisation is likely to collapse due to the conflict between the infinite demands and finite natural resources (Fearnside, 1986). The major influences of resettlements were the Muslim conquest of Northern Africa and the Christian re-conquest of Liberia (Thompson, 1978).

In summary, the biophysical environment and population factors have influenced the settlement and resettlement processes. The major influences include land degradation, natural hazards, and political and economic factors.

3.4.8 Human-induced factors

In pre-colonial Africa, ethnic conflict and slave trade forced people to settle on hilltops mainly for defence purposes (Kaloko, 1982). In the Jos plateau of Nigeria, for example, settlement sites were built in clusters, hidden by rocky ridges and surrounded by thorn and dense bushes to protect themselves from the slave traders, colonialists and from other outside forces (Pritchard, 1979: 124). Today, owing to regional conflicts, famine, political and religious conflicts, and population pressure on the available resources a great number of people, especially in various parts of Africa, are being forced to move and resettle in the previously avoided and climatically unfavourable zones, which are also infested with malaria and trypanosomiasis. Such areas are often also far removed from the original settlements.

As a result of wars, conflicts, resettlement and villagisation programmes, more than 2 million people from Ethiopia were forced to resettle mainly in the Sudan, Kenya, Djibouti, Western Europe and USA in the 1980s. Following the 1991 government change and the emergence of regional politics more than 450,000 Ethiopians were displaced and resettled in various urban centres and marginally classified rural areas of the country. In 1992, about 500,000 people from Somalia and 460,000 from the Sudan also resettled in eastern and south-western Ethiopia, respectively. In 1991, an estimated 500,000

Eritrean refugees were resettled in the Sudan and the recent war between Ethiopia and Eritrea (former province) forced thousands of people to resettle far from their original settlements.

3.4.9 External factors

External factors driving resettlement include such factors as the introduction of new rules and regulations, religion, marketing systems, land tenure programme, technology, crop, plant and animal species by outsiders. Due to the development of various infrastructures, new diseases can be transmitted and diffused by newcomers. These external factors can be associated with the resettlement processes, which cause people to abandon their original settlements. In the early 19th century owing to the improper demarcation of political boundaries by the colonial powers, a great number of people had to cross frontier zones and resettle in many parts of Africa.

For instance, several thousands of the Nuer people from the southern Sudan moved into Gambela where they have since resettled permanently (Pritchard, 1979). In order to control the people in 1956, the colonialists in Kenya forced 830,000 Kikuyus from the Kiambu, Muranga and Nyeri districts to resettle in the lowlands (HABITAT, 1986 and Mbithi et al., 1975). The colonialists also forced the indigenous people in Nigeria, Zimbabwe, Cameroon, Sierra Leone, among others, to resettle in the less fertile lowlands while the colonialists themselves settled in the best parts which had most of the arable land. Between 1830 and 1962, the French spread their settlements in most of the fertile lands in the coastal plains of Oran, Skikda, Annaba, and the Cheliff Valley and beyond the Tell Mountains in Algeria, and forced the natives to resettle in the infertile parts. During the War of Independence (1954-61), at least two million Algerians were resettled by the French Army under the emergency resettlement programme.

The other external factors are the introduction large-scale technological developments, for example, hydropower projects, commercial farms and logging of rain forest regions, which had forced people to abandon their original settlements. The construction of the Aswan High Dam in Egypt, the Sardar Sarovar and Farakka Dams in India, the Akosombo Dam on the Volta region in Ghana, the Gezira irrigation scheme in the Sudan, the new dam along the Yellow River in China (this dam is the largest in the world), among others, have forced people to abandon their original settlements in search of alternative places to live.

3.5 The Planned Resettlement Schemes

Most countries consider resettlement schemes as a strategy for alleviating environmental degradation, diffusion of technology, and minimising regional conflicts. Under the planned resettlement schemes there are the *voluntary* and *involuntary* types.

3.5.1 The voluntary resettlement schemes

A voluntary resettlement scheme is a process whereby people move to resettlement sites willingly. Such schemes manifest a more or less sound resettlement planning methodology through which the resettlers are well informed about the new resettlement sites as well as when and how they will be resettled. The success of the voluntary resettlement schemes depends often on the availability of resources, infrastructures and suitable environmental conditions.

During the founding of the State of Israel, the Jewish people established successful settlements voluntarily (Clout, 1979). The 1967 Arab-Israeli war changed the settlement patterns of the country. The Jewish people, who had migrated from different corners of the world to Israel, resettled in the central parts of the country, on the Golan Heights and in the Jordan Rift Valley (the West Bank) (Clout, 1979). After the collapse of communism and the introduction of a new policy in the ex-Soviet Union more than 33,000 Soviet Jews resettled in Israel and at least a million more are waiting to be resettled (The New York Times, 1991). The diffusion of the settlement sites changed significantly in their morphology of settlement patterns, and this aggravated the social conflicts between the Arabs and the Jewish people. This can be compared with the resettlement schemes in Sardinia, Italy, which were successful since they were accompanied by far-reaching land reform programmes (King, 1971).

In Burkina Faso, a large number of people moved from the more drought-prone and war-ridden agricultural regions of the country to the resettlement sites. They were ultimately successful in carrying out development programmes which resulted in higher income levels, initiation of road construction, strengthened social services and the development of on- and off-farm income-generating activities. However, the land tenure policy continued to aggravate the traditional conflict between the farmers and the pastoralists (McMillan, 1987).

Some lessons can be drawn from the Zimbabwe's resettlement schemes (The Economist, 1989:64), which were introduced by the post-independence government in 1980-81. The resettlement was designed to settle native families in the white-owned farmlands, which were abandoned during the war years. In 1982, 52,000 African families were resettled; the programme brought mixed results. Despite the long periods of drought, the resettlers produced more grain per hectare in comparison to the former white farmers. The reasons for this such success were: (a) the realistic agrarian policy, (b) the suitable farm technologies, (c) the peaceful implementation of the resettlement plan which led to the favourable pricing policies for the crops, and better access to health-care and education facilities.

But the resettlement scheme along the Volta River Valley, which was launched in the 1930s and again in the 1950s, brought little success due to the lack of understanding by the planners, as well as the physical and social constraints of the region. Since the 1950s, Rwandese refugees had begun to move to western Uganda and this led to ethnic and political conflicts. By 1980s and 1990s, the number of resettlers had reached 84,000 people. This population influx had given rise to four main problems, namely: (a) the Ugandan government did not have sufficient resources to give the services expected or required; (b) since the resettlers had occupied limited areas the human and livestock populations had increased considerably; (c) the biophysical and social crises had pushed the refugees to start armed conflicts with the Rwandan government; and (d) the incidence and range of human and animal diseases had increased (Foster, 1989).

3.5.2 The involuntary resettlement schemes

In an involuntary resettlement scheme, people are forced to move involuntarily. Military force is not necessarily used to achieve this. But the resetters are obliged to leave their original settlements because of the following reasons: (a) governments introduce new settlement plans which are not acceptable to the original settlers; (b) the traditional survival strategies of the local people are not sustainable and employment opportunities are not available; and (c) governments do not assist the local people since either they want to push out the people from their original settlements or they have financial constraints; and the resettlers do not have proper knowledge about the new resettlement areas.

The following examples of country cases are cited to illustrate the nature of the involuntary resettlement process.

In the nomadic pastoralist regions of Turkey, Iran, Syria and Egypt, forced resettlement programmes have been imposed by their respective governments, which in many respects showed disastrous results during the initial stages of the programmes (Hoyle, 1980). In the 1960s, some of the resettlers in the Kachia Grazing Reserve in Nigeria deserted their resettlement sites, due to their poor conditions. The Koinadugu Integrated Agricultural Development Project in Northern Sierra Leone succeeded in settling hundreds of peasants and nomads but failed to fulfil its goals because of certain problems: (a) the planners and project authorities did not understand the biophysical environmental systems; (b) the competition between herders and farmers and the conflict among different ethnic groups of herders over land-resources; (c) varied local economies; and (d) the adoption of the subsistence economy as a survival economy (Oxby, 1984).

Involuntary resettlement schemes were attempted between 1964 and 1977 in the Northern, Eastern, Central and Southern regions of Thailand, but had failed miserably owing to a number of factors: (a) the displacement of resettlement sites through the construction of the Phumiphol Dam and other hydroelectric projects; (b) lack of land reform policy; (c) involuntary resettlement process; (d) the absence of agricultural intensification; and (e) the subordination of the local and traditional interests to the colonial and institutional interests (Palmer, 1974 and Scudder, 1973).

Since the introduction of large-scale resettlement projects in the area of the Congo and Nile watershed of Rwanda in 1958, large forest areas have been destroyed. Between 1958 and 1979 in the Nyungwe area alone, the rain forest shrank from 114,000 to 97,000 hectares with a loss of more than 600 hectares in the border zones of the country. Large-scale development projects, financed by the World Bank and the European Development Bank, cleared the natural forests without reforestation, drained swampy areas and resettled thousands of people, mainly nomads. The loss of forest and swampy areas increased the rate of land degradation and the depletion of soil nutrients. Moreover, the resettlers had to face unexpected drought, floods, unhealthy climate and tropical diseases (Kleinert, 1987).

In 1975, the government of the Republic of Somalia, with the active assistance of the former Soviet Union, introduced a resettlement programme and as a result 120,000 nomadic Somalis were moved from the northern to the southern parts of the country. Although about half of them were said to have adopted a fishing economy and sedentary agricultural life-style, the remaining ones returned to their places of origin due to the problems of adapting to the new settled life (Olsson, 1976). The resettlement process in Somalia was similar to the one experienced in Ethiopia, which will be discussed later in this book. The main factors that accounted for resettlement in both countries were: (a) drought, famine and socialist ideology; (b) the movement of people was from the North to the South; (c) both governments attempted to resettle people far from their original settlements instead of creating incentives and improving the land resources in their original settlements; (d) the two governments were advised and assisted by the government of the former Soviet Union; and (e) due to lack of sufficient food, infrastructural and health-care facilities many people died, and others took refuge in other places. Although large-scale farming systems had been introduced they did not succeed owing to the centralised political systems and unfamiliarity with the mechanised farming systems introduced in the resettlement areas. The resettlement schemes in both countries were interrupted by the changes of governments since 1991. No clear alternative resettlement schemes have been introduced since then in these countries. Instead population displacements have continued due to war and ethnic conflicts.

In the Sudan, even though the resettlement schemes of Gezira, Managil, the Baraka, the Gash and the Gedaref were founded by involuntary means they have proved to be relatively successful. But many scholars believe that these schemes were not successful considering the continued problems of ecological destruction, poverty and lack of environmental awareness and proper planning.

The traditional scattered settlement pattern in Tanzania, as in other African countries, was adapted to the prevailing rural economy. It had an efficient method of environmental management without disturbing the ecological balance. Without understanding the role of the scattered settlement pattern, the German colonial administration forced people in some parts of the country to live in concentrated settlement sites. Religious missionaries also attracted people to resettle in the nucleated settlements. After independence, there were many landless and unemployed people in the urban areas. In response to this challenge, the Rural Settlement Commission in Tanzania established 23 resettlement sites and resettled more than 3400 families in the 1960s (Kikula, 1997). The massive and hasty resettlement programme, popularly known as Ujamaa Villagisation programme, was continued in 1970 and 1976 and involved the largest number of people in the history of the developing world. By 1978, the programme succeeded in resettling 82 percent of the rural population.

Unfortunately, critics of the Villagisation Programme have not been able to appreciate the positive aspects of this programme. Following the observations of this author, the resettlement process brought about both negative and positive effects if judged impartially. Under the Ujamaa Programme, both social and physical infrastructures were introduced, e.g. roads, water supply, education, health, marketing facilities etc. Afforestation, soil and water conservation programmes together with semi-zero grazing systems were introduced in some localities. At the same time there were also some negative effects of the Programme. Among these were deforestation, desertification, soil erosion, and declining crop yields. Hundreds of thousands of people returned to their original settlements, although some of them were later forced again to return to the planned resettlement sites. The reasons for the failure of the Programme were (a) the inadequacy of the basic natural resources, particularly farmland and water supply; (b) insufficient financial resources; (c) too much bureaucratisation; (c) involuntary resettlement; and (d) low level of land carrying capacity (Coulson, 1982; Muzo, 1983 and Kikula, 1997).

3.6 SUMMARY

How much can any resettlement scheme help to improve the well-being of the society and reduce the land-use and environmental problems? This depends largely on the short- and long-term policies available, the spatial distribution of the resettlement sites, the management of the natural resources, the financial strength, the level of technology and the administrative capacity of the institutions of the settlement schemes themselves.

The voluntary and involuntary resettlement processes have contributed neither to the alleviation of employment problems and poverty nor to the introduction of improved management systems. Previously sustainable traditional settlement systems were first disturbed during the colonial period and then during the post-colonial era through ill-planned agricultural projects, urban establishments and natural and man-made calamities. Although there were some successes through government assistance, in general the biophysical and social environmental costs have exceeded the benefits. Such costs include: (a) deforestation; (b) improper utilisation of resources; and (c) pollution, fires, floods, drought, hunger, diseases and deaths in most resettlement schemes. The issues that have not been addressed properly include: (a) land ownership; (b) the availability of agricultural land; (c) water and energy supplies; (d) the vulnerability of land to flood and landslide; (e) soil nutrients; (f) institutional credits; and (g) off-farm employment opportunities and medical facilities.

Voluntary resettlement schemes have not always been successful unless they have been supported by: locally-based improved planning systems; better balance between the regional distribution of people and land resources; effective land reform policy, especially in societies where land remains the most important economic asset, but the technology is inappropriate and the capital is scarce. For instance a study on the Chitwan and Nawlpus Resettlement Schemes (1953-54) in Nepal showed that a large number of the resettlers were landless and near landless even though the objectives of the schemes had provided for land availability. The main reason for this was that land was provided through influential people and nepotism (Shrestha, 1989).

In general, the experiences of many African and Latin American countries show that the planners failed to distribute sufficient land to the resettlers and showed lack of co-ordination among the government institutions (Chambers, 1969, and Nelson, 1977).

While the settlement process is as old as human history, the notion of planned resettlement is relatively new and it has been used as a development strategy in many parts of the world. The development of the planned settlement is associated with: (a) either the capitalist or socialist ideology; (b) pre-and post-colonial policies; (c) introduction of new technologies; (d) natural calamities; (e) high population growth in a limited area; (f) scarcity of crop and grazing lands; and (g) lack of employment opportunities. War and ethnic conflicts have resulted in increased need for human (re)settlement. However, most resettlement schemes have aggravated the existing problems, such as ethnic conflict, food shortage and deforestation. The biophysical, socio-economic and political environments have not enabled resettlers to become self-sufficient in food and the creation of employment opportunities. In fact, the success or failure of any planned (re)settlement programme depends largely on food and water availability, health care and the settlers' adaptation to the biophysical environment, to mention only the more important factors.

Although environmental crises are global phenomena their causes, extent, effects and solutions vary from region to region. The environmental crises in Sub-Saharan Africa contribute greatly to the present economic and political instability, land-use conflicts, and shortages of health facilities, food and water supplies. Rapid population growth and low agricultural outputs aggravate all these. None of the measures proposed to solve these problems have been found to be workable. As long as the African villages and hamlets remain fragmented without being brought together under planned resettlement schemes, sustainable use of the resources cannot be realisable. Therefore, without sufficient and coherent planned resettlement programmes, human and biophysical rehabilitation measures cannot be taken in the sub-tropical, tropical, humid-and sub-humid regions of Africa.

4 CHAPTER 4: THE EFFECTS OF THE SETTLEMENT AND RESETTLEMENT PROCESSES ON THE BIOPHYSICAL AND HUMAN ENVIRONMENTS IN ETHIOPIA

This Chapter deals with the effects of the pre-and post-1980s non-planned and planned resettlements in the northern and southern parts of the country on the biophysical and human landscape features in Ethiopia. It also describes the population relocation process following the 1991 change of government.

Altitude and relief mainly influence the spatial distribution of settlement patterns in Ethiopia, which are in turn affected by temperature and precipitation. Based on the elevation, temperature, and natural vegetation and moisture criteria the country is divided into three main physiographic regions, namely: the north-eastern highlands and associated lowlands, the south-western highlands and associated lowlands; and the Ethiopian Rift Valley.

For the purpose of this book, the physiographic regions have been generalised into two major thermal and altitudinal zones, namely the highlands (>1,500 m) and the lowlands (<1500 m) (Mesfin, 1970 & 1972, Griffiths, 1972 and Daniel, 1983).

Ethiopia is located wholly within the tropics. This means that every part of the country can see the overhead sun twice a year. But as Ethiopia is a mountainous country the high tropical temperature is greatly modified by altitude. This indicates that with an increase in altitude there is a corresponding decrease in temperature.

The relationships between altitude and temperature in Ethiopia result in the following local temperature zones: (a) *Kurr or wurch* – >3,300 m (the highland ecological zone). The mean annual temperature is 10 °C or less; (b) *Dega* – 2, 300 m to about 3, 300 m (the highland ecological zone). The mean annual temperature is between 10 and 15 °C or less; (c) *Woyna dega* - 1,500 m to about 2,300 m (the highland ecological zone). The mean annual temperature is between 15 and 20 °C; (d) *Kola* - 500 to 1, 500 m. Hot temperature (about 30 °C) (lowland ecological zone); and (e) *Berha* – less than 500 m (lowland ecological zone); very hot temperature (39 to 40 °C). Although the highlands cover only about 40 percent of the total area of the country, 88% of the population, 60% of the livestock and 90% of the agriculturally suitable area are concentrated in the highland areas (Daniel, 1983).

As a result, 50% of the highland is significantly eroded and the rest is relatively free from serious erosion (Aggrey-Mensha, 1988; Samuel, 1985, FAO, 1986). The degradation of the biophysical landscape is due to the long history of population resettlement, over-cultivation, over-grazing and deforestation. Most of the lowlands have a hot dry or humid temperature and are characterised by tropical diseases, irregular and low rainfall, sparse vegetation and population with few permanent settlements, even though several new resettlements have been established since the 1970s and 1980s. Mesfin (1988) contends that the lowlands are more vulnerable to any types of land-use change than the highlands although this area covers about 60% of the total of the country. Though some original settlements were affected by the post-1970s policy-induced Resettlement Programmes the following resettlement morphologies are still commonly found in Ethiopia.

4.1 Ethiopia's Resettlment Morphologies

The spatial distribution of languages, religions, ethnic groups, agricultural development and political activities reflect the history of resettlement processes. The resettlement morphology (forms, types and patterns), location and sites are affected by historical, spatial and environmental factors. Based on surveys made by Last (1977) and Stitz (1970), the (re)settlement morphologies are classified into nucleated; closely spaced; dispersed widely spaced and pastoral-nomadic settlement types.

4.1.1 Nucleated or compact resettlements

The nucleated settlement type, shown in Figure 4, is one of the most widespread settlement types in the *woyna dega* agro-ecological zone. In this type of settlement, houses are closely related or compact, and are inhabited by an extended family. Such resettlement morphologies are common in the highland regions of western Tigray, Achefer, Ylmana Densa in Gojam, Wogera, Dembia and Alefa-Takussa in Gondar, western and central Wello, northern and southern Shewa (e.g. in Merhabete), Konso in Gamo Gofa, etc.). Such (re)settlement pattern could have been transferred into agricultural-based urban centre if resettlement and villagisation programmes were planned properly.

Figure 4. A nucleated or compact resettlement type (Dejen, Gojam, 1988)

4.1.2 Closely spaced settlements

In the southern part of the country, especially in the "hoe culture" or *enset* (false banana) zone with other different annual and perennial crops, houses or homesteads are closely spaced. Villagers in these types of settlement mostly have strong social and economic ties, although some of them have lost their ties.

4.1.3 Widely spaced settlements

This settlement type consists of widely spaced groups of dwellings located on hilltops, which are demarcated by physical features such as rivers and steep valleys. These settlements are also found in forest areas and at the margins of wetlands or hills. Stitz (1970) described this type of resettlement as being loosely connected and linear.

4.1.4 Dispersed settlements

Dispersed settlements are found in the areas bordering the lowlands, the highlands and alluvial soil environments along the banks of the major rivers. In this type of settlement the compounds are scattered and they are not socially cohesive.

Households in this type of dispersed settlement depend mainly on their own plots and use traditional technology (e.g. hoe), which is suitable to the types of farming system and produce mainly perennial crops.

4.1.5 Pastoral-nomadic settlements

Pastoral-nomadic settlements have closely-grouped homesteads which are located adjacent to water-wells or streams. They are made of either temporary or semi-permanent structures. The pastoral-nomads can abandon these areas as soon as the basic economic resources (grass and water) are exhausted. These settlements portray territorial kinship relationships rather than morphological similarities. Nevertheless, some pastoralist groups, like the Afars, have adapted to the clustered resettlement (*Gaanta*) morphology. This type of resettlement is suited to the Middle Awash-Valley along the Awash River and watering-points. Usually the number of huts *(Bura)* in a settlement is more than 20. Similar settlement sites are also observed in the Lower Awash Valley. The settlement sizes in the Borana pastoralist areas vary from a few houses to over 30.

4.1.6 Centralised/nucleated settlements

In addition to the above stated (re)settlement types, there are central (re)settlements, starting from the historical Emperor's camps and churches. The archaeological evidence in Axum indicates that the settlement pattern that emerged during the early, middle and late Axumite periods was of the nucleated type. This type of resettlement has extended to most parts of the Tigrinya speaking highlands (i.e. the Eritrean-Tigrian highlands). The present nucleated settlement pattern in Lalibela and Gondar towns had its roots in the Emperor's camps of the 12th and 17th centuries respectively. These settlements were later transformed into large permanent royal family settlements and eventually into town settlements. In the late 1870s, Emperor Menilek set up royal camps on Mount Wuchacha in Shewa, but he soon moved northwards and established his camp near the summit of the Entoto Mountain. The choice of this site was determined by strategic considerations. There he built his palace and the Entoto Mariam church. Later he moved his palace to Finfinne in Addis Ababa, because of the natural hot springs favoured by Empress Taitu (Trimingham, 1952 and Lewis, 1985).

Similar nucleated settlements are also found elsewhere in the country. In the northern and central highlands, churches and monasteries were built near palaces and castles. Church settlements can easily be identified from a distance since they are located on high altitudes associated with valuable trees of *Juniperus procera* within their compounds. In any church settlement the number of houses varies from two in local churches to more than 500 in monasteries. Waldba and Mahbere Selassie (Gondar); Aba Aregawy and Debre Damo (Tigray); Ziquala Abo and Debre Libanos (Shewa) and Wegeg Asobot *Gedam* (Hararge) are some of the monastery settlements in the country.

4.2 Factors Influencing Settlement Patterns

The following factors are believed to be the main reasons that explain the patterns, structure and forms of the settlement types discussed above. These factors include relief, climate and soil. The *woyna dega* climatic zone has a greater influence on settlements than the *kola* climatic zone and poor drained black soils. In order to minimise physical distance from the settlement sites to the various economic resource sites many farmers settle in a dispersed manner over the landscape. Strategic considerations, kinship ties, availability of natural and local economic resources, land-tenure systems and close family relationships contribute to the concentration of settlements. Such settlements are often built by groups of peoples who claim common ancestry.

What is important to note here is that on the one hand the land tenure systems oblige the farmers to settle together and on the other hand members of the same ethnic group are forced to settle in a scattered manner in view of population increase and the variation of soil types and the topography of the areas. Stitz (1970) in his study of northern Shewa observed that there were farmers who had moved from the nucleated settlements and resettled in dispersed farmsteads located in areas that had fertile soils. There were also others who were forced to resettle in areas with less fertile soils due to the threat from robbers and to avoid land fragmentation and the spread of diseases. Mesfin (1972) argued that the larger the average size of the farm the more scattered the settlements are and the smaller the average farm size the more compact settlements become.

In most of the lowland areas, slash and burn-cultivation methods and hunting-gathering economies have forced the people to settle in dispersed settlement patterns. The availability and shortage of water, which are indispensable for the pastoral-nomadic way of life in the lowlands, has obliged the population to live in dispersed settlements and change their settlements seasonally.

Since 1985, most traditional villages in the highland regions were turned by government decree into planned villages under the nation-wide villagisation programme (Cohen et al., 1987, Dejene, 1990).

Through this policy more than 25 million people were resettled until the collapse of the socialist regime of Ethiopia in 1991. Although the number of houses in a nucleated village varied from place to place, this author counted between100 and 300 houses. Even the Borana pastoral people were forced to live in the new villages. What must be noted here is that the clustered settlements of the pre-1970s were formed through voluntary means and were self-managed mostly. But the post-1980s resettlements were created involuntary through government plans. The indigenous groups of peoples include pastoral nomads, shifting cultivators, hunter-gatherers and settled farmers. The term indigenous peoples describe those social groups with a cultural identity that is distinct from that of the dominant society. This identity makes them vulnerable and disadvantaged in the development process (World Bank, 1991).

The pastoral nomads who own large numbers of livestock produce either very little grain or none at all. Most of them are forced to live in the semi-arid areas and have the same settlement patterns, which are not permanent. The shifting cultivators inhabit the tsetse fly-infested western and south-western parts of the lowland regions. They use rudimentary tools like hoes and produce subsistence crops. They change their settlements whenever their plots of land are exhausted. Most of the hunter-gatherers reside along the major rivers basin systems and are engaged in hunting wild animals and gathering wild fruits, honey and root-crops, although some of them also practise shifting cultivation. The settled farmers work on the large-scale state and private farms located in the lowland areas. Presently about 15% of the population are settled in the small, medium and large urban areas. But most of the settlements are rural towns.

Peasants who depend entirely on livestock and crop farming (e.g. mixed farming) settle in the highland areas. This signifies that the highland farmers who have large livestock populations produce a considerable amount of grain while the lowland farms that have large livestock populations produce limited quantities of grain. Since the large livestock populations constitute the economic base for the lowlands they require large grazing lands which are not available in the highland regions. In view of the prevalence of diseases and aridity in the lowlands the population density is small with an average of six persons per square kilometre.

The push factors in the highlands include population pressure, farmland fragmentation, land degradation and incidence of famine and wars. Owing to the pull factors such as trade, the expansion of communications, commercial farms and the opportunities for wage labour, many people have resettled in the western, south-western and southern lowlands of the country. Figure 5 demonstrates the relationship between the spatial distribution of human resettlements and the biophysical environment.

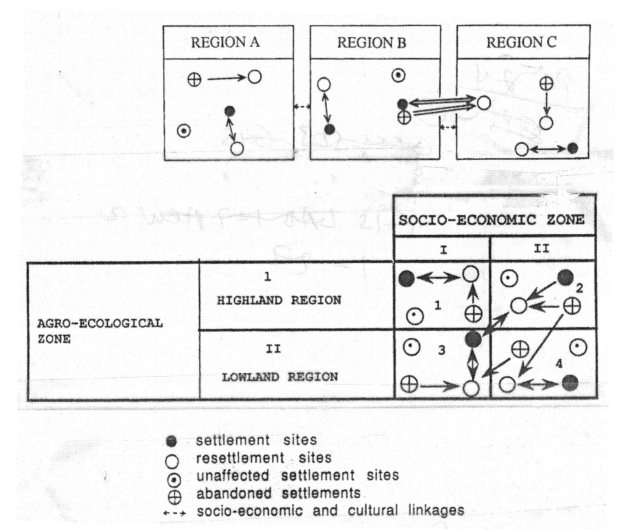

Figure 5. Relationship between spatial population distribution, the highland and lowland geographical regions.

The above figure indicates that there is a movement of people from one type of agro-ecological and socio-economic zone in the highland region to the lowland regions or vice versa. It also shows the movement of people within the southward and northward resettlement processes and between and among (re)settlement sites. Such (re)settlement processes took many decades and occurred during different seasons of the year. For example, in Region 1, the push factors seemed less powerful than the ones in Regions 2 and 3. Unlike in Region 1, in Region 4 people who abandoned their original settlements resettled outside the demarcated areas. But those who had once moved from Region 2 to Region 4 and from Region 4 to Region 3 returned to their original resettlements. The movements between and within the different agro-ecological and cultural zones occur through both the non-planned and planned resettlements.

4.3 The Non-Planned Resettlements

This section attempts to present the southward and northward population movements that occurred in the historical past under the various agro-ecological zones, and political and socio-economic systems. Prior to the 1950s, two major non-planned took place both in southward and northward directions (Wood, 1977, see also Mengistu 1995b). The major push factors for the southward and northward non-planned (re)settlement processes were the need for the control of land resources. The movements towards the different ecological zone are discussed below:

4.3.1 The southward non-planned resettlements

The earliest (re)settlement have been found in the vicinity of Axum, Tigray, and elsewhere in northern Ethiopia, and at Adulis in Eritrea before the fifth century B.C. At that time the Beja pastoralists had settled in the area north of the Barka-Ansaba River Basin. The Agaw had settled in the region south of the Marab Beles and Jema Rivers, and the Kunama-Barya had occupied the area between the (re)settlement regions of the Beja and the Agaw. By the sixth century some of the Agaw people of the north had resettled in western Gojam. The kings of Axsum extended their rule and controlled the land and water resources around the port of Zeila in the Red Sea, the Saho territory in the south and the Beja plateau in the north (in Eritrea). Later the Muslim-Arabs were attracted by the resources along the Red Sea coast. As a result, they converted the local peoples from Ethiopia and Somalia to Islam in the 12th century. Due to population pressure and drought, the Muslim pastoralists from Somalia moved and resettled along the fertile land of Wabe Shebele River Basin in Ethiopia and they, in turn, converted many people to Islam (Trimingham, 1952). Through the expansion of Islam in Ethiopia, Christian Aksum lost its trade-links with the Mediterranean world and as a result its kings were forced to move to Lasta in Wello in the 13th century, and much later to Gondar (Lewis, 1985). Amde Syon (1314-1344) countered the Muslim expansion with the invasion of large areas in the eastern and southern parts of the country and converted many people to Christianity as well as building settlements such as churches and palaces. However, the expansion of the settlements was interrupted both by internal and external forces. In order to defend Islam, the Ottoman Turks invaded and established (re)settlement sites at Massawa and Harkiko in the 1500s. When the Abyssinian kingdom was weakened the Muslims of Adal (Afar), who were assisted by the Ottoman Turks, built (re)settlements along the Awash-Valley and in some other parts of Ethiopia in 1530 (Levine, 1974). The Portuguese in the name of Christianity established (re)settlements at Massawa and the island of Socotra in the entrance of the Red Sea in the 16th century. The struggle between the Portuguese and the Ottoman Turks over the land resources and commercial routes to the Arabian Sea and the sea routes to India brought about resource degradation and stagnation (Trimingham, 1952, see also Mengistu, 1995b). The above mentioned factors were responsible for the southward movement of the people.

4.3.2 The northward non-planned resettlement

The Oromo people are among the most expansive societies on record in Africa (Asmerom, 1973). The Oromo lived in the relatively arid environment along the southern border of the Ethiopian plateau and the northern part of present-day Kenya before they moved to the heartland of the country in the 16th century (Abir, 1980). Before the Oromo moved along the three river basins of Ganale, Galana Duli and Galana Sagan, the Borana and Guji pastoralists settled these areas. In the fifteenth century, the Oromo developed the Gada system, which was later imposed on the people in the conquered territories. Had the Gada system been maintained the present rapid population growth and the accompanying deforestation would have been minimised.

The (re)settlement movement started after the conquest of many regions by Ibrahim al-Ghazi (1506-1543), nicknamed "Gran" or the 'left-handed'. He was helped by the Ottoman Turks and converted many Oromo pastoralists to Islam. As the two Ethiopian historians, Azazh T'ino and Bahrey have written, the Oromo pastoralists first moved from their original settlements in the Ethiopian Rift Valley towards the Genale River and invaded Bale by 1522. Thereafter between 1546 and 1562 some of the Oromos moved towards the south, south-west and west. Another group migrated to the east, central and northern highlands in 1562 and continued to live in these areas until the 18th century (Cited from Alemeida by Bahrey1954). During this invasion, the Oromo culture dominated not only the cultures of Borana-Guji, the kingdoms of Bale, Fattagar, Hadia, Dwaro, Sidama and Gurage but also interfered in the Amhara-Tigray cultures (Asmerom, 1973, Taddesse, 1972). Despite the subsequent history and the Oromo domination by the Amharas in Ethiopia, some Oromos, particularly the Yeju dynasty, achieved great political power. Through these processes the Oromo settlers became agriculturalists by learning from the highland Amharas and Tigrays, and some were converted to Christianity (Levine, 1974). Others became members of the ruling class and changed the ancient name Lako Malza to Wello (Stitz, 1970, Tayya, 1922).

While the Muslim Oromos were ruling and expanding their settlement sites in most parts of the country, another Amhara-Tigrean resettlement process started under Emperor Tewedros (1845-1860); Yohannes (1863-1881) and Menilek (1889-1913). This process took place in the southern, south-western and eastern parts of Ethiopia. From the 1870s onwards the Amharas and Tigreans established resettlement sites and a significant number of the Oromos joined forces with them. Through the processes of intermarriage, language and religious adaptations took place (Levine, 1974: 84-85).

Finally it can be contended that population pressure on the resources, unsustainable technological development and climatic factors were the main reasons that accounted for the northward population movement.

The Oromos' original resettlement regions were hot with irregular rainfall and low moisture (Daniel, 1983) and were infested with animal and human diseases. Because of this and other factors the pastoralists were pushed to new lands beyond their territory. The Oromo resettlements, especially in the central and northern highland regions, contributed to over-overgrazing, deforestation and soil erosion, which became the main causes for the northward population movement. As a result, a new administrative structure, unjust land tenure system, agricultural marketing and trading systems were imposed upon the local peoples such as the Kambatas, Hadyas and Wolaitas (Levine, 1974). Between the 1950s and 1970s, short- and long-distance non-planned (re)settlement processes took place both within and between regions. Long distance refers to a physical distance of more than 150 km while short distance refers to less than 50 km (Wood, 1977). It is estimated that over one million people resettled spontaneously in the various parts of the country (Wood, 1985). The major push factors for such non-planned resettlements were: land degradation, poor economic conditions, unjust land tenure systems, and the introduction of commercial farms with surplus labour in slack seasons of the year. Resettlements between and within regions were a traditional survival strategy. Until recently it was a tradition that people from the densely populated and drought-affected areas of Tigray and Wello would move freely to Gondar and Gojam in search of food and employment opportunities. Later, some returned to their original settlements but others resettled in the new areas and adapted to the new environment. In this respect three types of resettlers were observed: (a) the pastoralists and the subsistence farmers who resettled and occupied grazing and agricultural land by travelling long- and short- distance; (b) the subsistence farmers who resettled and occupied agricultural land after travelling a relatively short distance (<50 km) from their homesteads; and (c) the subsistence farmers who resettled after having travelled long distances (>150 km) and became labourers on the commercial farms (Wood, 1985). However, these traditional survival strategies have been negatively affected by various government policies, which have led to ethnic conflicts and degradation of natural resources.

Since most parts of the northern highlands produce only one crop a year, due to the nature of the rainy season, labourers could move to the southern and south-western highland regions of the country during the 'slack' dry season. The number of labourers required in these regions was determined by: (a) the increasing number of absentee landlords who owned forest land to develop coffee farms; (b) high coffee prices following the Second World War; (c) population increase in the highland (sending) regions; (d) the development of road transport which linked both the sending and receiving regions; (e) a growing number of urban unemployed who sought employment opportunities elsewhere; and (f) the desire of some nomadic pastoralists to resettle as cultivators.

4.3.3 Emergency and forced resettlements

Various types of forced resettlement have occurred from the ancient times up to the early nineteenth century (Pankurst, 1982). For example, when the Beja tribe rebelled against the Axumite Kingdom in the fourth century, King Ezana forced more than 4000 Bejas to resettle in Begemdir (Dembya, Gondar region), which is some distance to the south – south of the Tekeze river.

Over the last century, particularly after the Second World War, thousands of pastoralists and farmers were forced to resettle elsewhere due to the construction of hydroelectric power stations, the introduction of commercial farms, changed in land tenure systems and the natural disasters of the Kara Kore and Serdo earthquakes, drought, famine and wars (Gouin, 1972). Two striking examples are the Falasha, resettled in Israel, and the Konso people. Because of political unrest, degradation of land resources and prolonged poverty, in 1984/85 about 30,000 Falasha were taken out of the country through "Operation Moses" and resettled in Israel (Detroit Free Press, 1991). Some of the Konso people who lived in the higher altitudes of the Gamo Gofa region were resettled mainly in the Yanda Plain (Kloos et al., 1990).

4.4 The Planned Resettlements

Between 1950s-1980s a number of *voluntary* and *involuntary,* long- and short- distance planned resettlements took place in the various parts of the country. For the various types of settlement and spatial distribution in the different geographical regions are outlined in Table 2. The issue of planned (re)settlement was mentioned in the First Five Year Plan (1957-61) of the country (Ethiopian Government, 1967). Accordingly the first resettlement programme was established in 1959 at Abela (in

Sidamo region) which accommodated 700 farmers from the populated upland areas. Due to the development of commercial farms in the Awash-Valley, the Afar pastoralists lost their grazing and water rights (Assefa, 1964). As a result the then government resettled 20,000 pastoralists elsewhere within the Valley in Amibara in the Middle-Upper Awash Valley (Abdul Hamid, 1988). In 1960, army veterans were resettled in Awasa and some landless peoples from Menz and Sega Meda areas were resettled in Arba Minch. The Welamo Agricultural Development Unit (WADU) undertook similar types of resettlement programmes in 1965, which resettled 1,000 evicted families. In the same year, the Chillalo Agricultural Development Unit (CADU) also resettled 200 evicted farmers in Abomsa, Arsi region in 1965. Thousands of the urban unemployed and young school dropouts were also resettled in the Upper Gibe Valley in the 1970s (Last, 1977; Wood, 1977: 75-77).

RECEIVING REGIONS	SENDING REGIONS	YEAR	C.P.R.	I.P.R.	P.P.R.
AWASH VALLEY	Adjacent areas of Wello, Shewa, Hararge, Menz and Gishe	1960s	0	0	4
GAMU GOFA (Arba Minch)	Menz and Gishe	1960s 1980s	0 3	0 3	1 0
SIDAMO (Abela, Awassa)	Addis Ababa and adjacent highlands of Sidamo	19509s	0 2	3 0	0 0
ARSI (Abomsa)	Farmers and pastoralists within the region	1980s	1	0	0
BALE (Harawa/Melka Oda)	From the adjacent areas of Bale and outside the region	1970s 1980s	0 2	0 0	1 0
WELLEGA (Assosa, Harogudru, Kelem, Nekemte, Arjo and Gimbi)	Areas from the north* and Shewa regions**	1970s 1980s	0 8	4 0	0 0
GONDAR (Settit Humera and Chilga)	Libo and Gaynt (Gondar) and in some places of Tigray region	1970s	0 2	1 0	0 0
SHEWA (Chebo-Gurage and Awash Valley)	Evicted pastoralists and farmers within the regions and from Wello region	1970s 1980s	0 3	0 3	1 0
KEFA (Gimira, Kefa, Dima and Lima)	Farmers within the region and from the north*	1980s	0	9	0
ILLUBABOR (Gore, Metu, Gambela and Buno-Bedele)	From the north* and Shewa regions**	1980s	5	4	0
GOJAM (Metekel)	Mota and Bichena (eastern Gojam, from Tigray, Wello* and Shewa*)	1980s	2	1	0
HARARGE	Gode and along the Awash Valley	1970s 1980s	0	0	7

Table 2: Receiving and Sending Regions between the 1960s and 80s

Note: Words in bracket are receiving areas within the regions. * Areas from the north include Rayya Azebo, Enderta, Mekele, Agame, Adwa, Shire and Tembien in Tigray Region; and Kalu, Borena Wereilu, Dessie Zuria, Ambassel, Yeju, Raya Kobo, Wadla-Delanta and Lasta Wag in Wello Region. ** Areas in Shewa Region include Kambata/Hadya, Menz and Gishe, Yefat, Temuga and Merhabete. C.P.R.=Conventional or Special Planned Resettlement. I.P.R.= Integrated Planned Resettlement. P.P.R.= Pastoral or Low-Cost Planned Resettlement
Source: Wood, 1977; Kloos, 1990, and field observations.

Following the 1974 Ethiopian Revolution, different types of (re)settlement programmes have been introduced. Because of the 1975 Land Reform Proclamation the government took the responsibility of jointly resettling peasants (PMAC, 1975). The planned resettlements were of two types, namely: the low-cost planned resettlement, and the special planned resettlement. The former was established mainly in State Farm areas and the latter in the peasant and pastoral areas. The resettlers benefited from the infrastructure and machinery that were available at the farm sites. The resettlers were organised into Peasant Associations (PAs) and were encouraged to engage in the socialist forms of co-operative ventures or principles (Mengistu, 1986). They were allowed to cultivate specified land holdings individually.

Between 1975 and 1983, the Resettlement Authority and the Relief and Rehabilitation Commission (RRC) resettled 110,090 persons on 88 different resettlement sites: Setit-Humera in Gondar, Gode in Hararge, Assosa Angergutin in Wellega and Harawa-Melka Oda in Bale were some of the resettlement areas (RRC, 1985, Jansson et al., 1987). The types of resettlers were unemployed people from the urban areas (19%), landless peasants (15%), war victim pastoralists (27%), and peasants suffering from famine and drought disasters (31%) (Dagnew, 1986) and the rest (8%) from other sources. The programme was disrupted between 1979 and 1983 due to the difficulty of managing the resettlement schemes and many resettlers were unwilling to remain in the new sites (Dawit, 1989). For the evolution of resettlement policies, see also Dessalegn, 2003.

The resettlers were transported to the new residence sites by the RRC, which was mandated by the government to provide them with food, seeds, technical support, credit, buildings, agricultural machinery and other inputs until they became self-supporting (RRC, 1985). A Special Resettlement Scheme was planned with the aim of the resettlers gaining self-sufficiency in a period of three years. However, this plan or scheme did not materialise as intended. The major reasons for the failure were: (a) the resettlement sites were not chosen properly in terms of the availability of fertile soils, water and health facilities; (b) resettlers were moved without being accompanied by their families and their household possessions; (c) the resettlement administrative costs, estimated at USD 3,600 per family per year, were very high; (d) the resettlers were not given the opportunity to decide for themselves; and (e) the pastoralists were unwilling to loose contact with their livestock (Abdul Hamid, 1988).

In 1984, the Government restarted resettlement activities. The main objectives of the 1984 Planned Resettlement Programme were to: (a) resettle 1.5 million rural population affected by drought, famine and war; (b) make use of the land and water resources for development purposes; (c) achieve self-sufficiency with respect to food and income generating activities in a three years period; and (d) introduce certain physical and social infrastructures (PMAC, 1984). The resettlement plan was considered to be the only remedy for the many problems faced by the country.

The previous socialist government of Ethiopia introduced two types of large-scale resettlement programmes, namely: The Planned Resettlement Programme known as *Sefera* and the Villagisation Programme known as the *Mender Misreta*. Under the Villagisation Programme 35% of the total peasant population (i.e. 47 million) were resettled in nucleated villages by 1988 (Alemayehu, 1989). Under the Villagisation Programme, the peasant farmers were resettled within their homesteads while under the Planned Resettlement Programme they were located at new sites that were 800 km or more from their original settlements. Under the Planned Resettlement Programme more than 600,000 peasants were moved from their densely populated areas to the lowland regions with altitudes <1500 m a.s.l. (Ministry of Agriculture, 1988). See Figure 6 and Table 3.

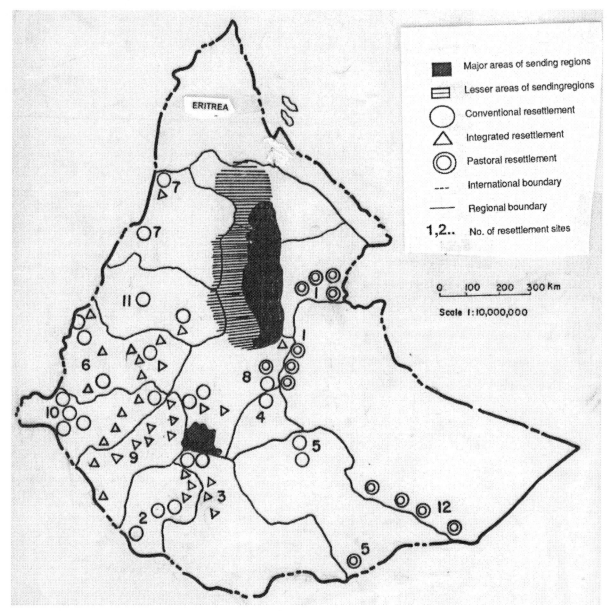

Figure 6. Planned resettlement between 1975 and 1991

Note: 1.Wello & Hararge; 2. Gamu Gofa; 3. Sidamo; 4. Arsi; 5. Bale; 6. Wollega; 7. Gondar; 8. **Shewa;** 9. Kefa; 10. Illubabor; 11. Gojam; 12. Hararge & Ogaden.
Sources: Wood, 1977 & 1983 and Kloos, 1990.

Table 3. Numbers of resettlers by sending and receiving regions

Receiving Regions			Sending Regions					
Regions	Settlers	%	Wello	%	Shewa	%	Tigray	%
Wollega	253,282	42.7	220,636	87.1	11,279	4.4	21,367	8.4
Illubabor	146,216	24.7	72,226	49.4	28,275	26.2	45,715	31.2
Gojam*	101,122	17.1	29,839	29.5	54,858	54.2	-	-
Kefa	79,838	13.4	50,690	63.5	6,514	8.1	22,634	28.3
Gondar**	6,397	1.1	-	-	-	100.0	-	-
Shewa	6,149	1.0	-	-	6,149	-	-	-
Total	593,004	100	373,392	63.0	107,075	18.1	89,716	15.2

* The total of 101,122 settlers in Gojam includes 16,425 (16.2%) resettled from within the same region.
** All resettlers in Gondar were resettled within the region.
Source: Pankhurst, 1992:56.

Since 1984, new resettlement patterns (Conventional Resettlement) replaced the former Special Planned Resettlement Programme or *Medebegna Sefera*. Similarly, the Integrated Resettlement or *Sigsega* and Pastoral Resettlement also replaced the former Low-Cost Planned Resettlement Programme.

The Conventional Resettlement sites accounted for about 55% of the total resettlement areas. The major receiving regions included: Wollega, Illubabor, Western Gojam and Gondar. The majority of the resettlers came from Central Wello, Tigray, Eastern Gojam and Gondar, and Northern and Southern Shewa. Most of the resettlers went to Gambela (Illubabor), Assosa (Wellega) and Metekel (Gojam) (RRC, 1985). The Conventional Resettlements were administered on the principles of co-operative farms. The members contributed their labour and received their share of the produce on a point system. See also on page 68. Every farm household had 0.1 ha plot of land. Owing to the large number of resettlers the population density figures changed from 2.8% per sq. km to 5 in Gambela (Illubabor); from 7.8 to 10.4 in Metekel (Gojam) and 15.6 to 18.9 in Assosa (Wollega) in the periods between 1984/85 and 1990/92. See Pankhurst, 1992.

The Integrated Resettlement Programme accounted for about 43% of the total resettlement areas and was located in the highland region. The peasant farmers were resettled within the existing PAs and were allotted land and oxen to till individually. A PA was selected for the integrated resettlement programme if the area was much larger than the number of households therein (RRC, 1981).

The pastoral resettlers represented about 2% of the total resettlers and were located within their grazing ecological zones in Bale, Hararge and Shewa Regions.

Through the mobilisation of university staff and students, and the employees of the various government institutions and organisations, about 1,440,000 people were generally forced to move out of the Administrative Regions of Wello, Tigray and South Shewa and were resettled in the various regions of the country (see Table 3). These people were forced out of their original settlement areas as a result of drought and famine. In most cases, the central government assigned quotas to the sending administrative regions.

These ambitious and mostly impractical resettlement schemes incurred great financial, material and human costs for the government. In order to implement these programs, over 13,000 campaigners from the institutions of higher learning, 25,000 employees from the government institutions and mass organisations as well as 2,259 cadres were deployed in 1984/85 (Clarke, 1987). The government made provisions with regard to transport, agricultural implements, shelter and the like. The government allocated 822 tractors in the conventional resettlement areas and 27,985 farm oxen in the integrated resettlement areas as well as six million kilograms of seeds, among other items of support. As a result, 110,000 hectares of forest and bush land were cleared to make way for the resettlements in the same year.

The then government expended an estimated total of 258 million Eth.Birr (2.50 Eth.Bir = was 1.00 USD) on the Resettlement Schemes for the period 1985 to 1988. Moreover, in terms of human costs the country lost a considerable number of teaching staff and students, farmers and other government employees mostly due to the tropical diseases, particularly malaria.

The chief factors for the introduction of the 1984 resettlement programme were:
- the 1975 land reform programme, the 1977 Ethio-Somali conflict over the Ogaden Region.
- the 1984-1985 famine.
- the establishment of the RRC and the Resettlement Authority; shortage of arable land in many of the original settlement areas.
- the establishment of mass organisations such as Peasant and Urban Dwelling Associations.

The post-1991 population relocation and resettlement policy differs significantly from the pre-1991. In the 1974-1991 periods resettlement programmes were mostly involuntary and forced, whereas in the post-1991 period voluntary resettlement was said to be used.

4.4.1 The relocation of people

Since 1991, thousands of people have been relocated and resettled. The relocation of people seems to be caused by the following factors:
- The collapse of the Socialist State and establishment of ethnic-based regional state administration systems.
- Lack of government assistance in the pre-1991 resettlement areas.
- Human-induced environmental deterioration.
- Food insecurity situation in different parts of the country.

Following the seizure of power by the Tigray Peoples Liberation Front (TPLF) in 1991, Ethiopia was divided into 14 Regions known locally as *killils* (see Figure 7). The Regional Administration Policy was first introduced by the Transitional Government of Ethiopia and later was approved by the Federal Democratic Republic of the country.

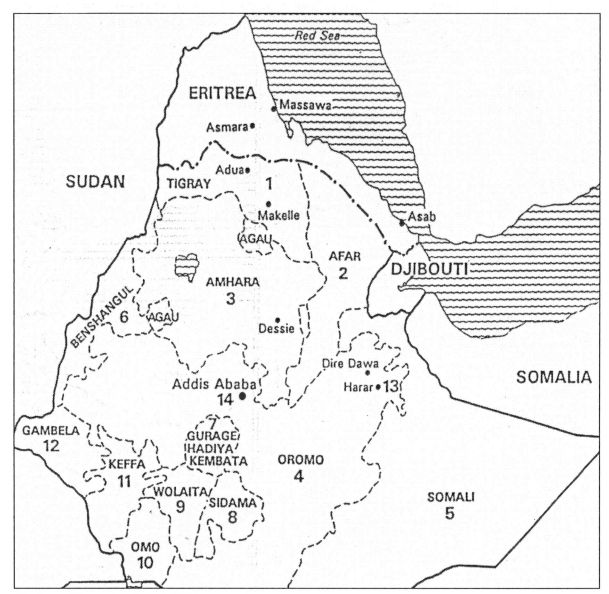

Figure 7. The 14 Regions (Killils)

When the former socialist government collapsed, the resettled abandoned their government sponsored resettlement areas since they lacked material and logistic support from the new government. They were also not protected from being attacked by ethnically aroused anti-resettlements and Villagisation sentiments during the transitional period. This disturbing situation forced thousands of people to resettle either in the already crowded urban areas or return to their ancestral places. In addition, inter-ethnic conflicts in the eastern, southern and south-western parts of the country contributed to the relocation of many people. These people returned to the already densely settled areas in Wello, Tigray and Shewa. This large influx of population aggravated fragmentation of farmland, land insecurity, land-use conflicts, environmental degradation and shortage of energy in many rural and urban areas.

As soon as the TPLF and EPLF (Eritrean People Liberation Front) forces entered Addis Ababa and Asmara, respectively, in 1991, it was estimated that some 300,000 soldiers were demobilised. The great majority of them were dislocated and resettled in their original homelands, which increased pressure on the land. Many of the resettled people could not stay in the rural areas so they migrated to the towns. For example one survey carried out both in Addis Ababa and Gondar in 1996-97 showed a severe housing shortage, which resulted in the creation of large-sized squatter settlements with the accompanying high crime rates, environmental pollution and diseases (Mengistu & Sjöberg, 1999).

The Ethio-Eritrean war has also brought about population dislocation. At least 350,000 Tigreans were forced out of Eritrea to resettle within Tigray. Similarly, in 1998, about 70,000 Eritreans were forced out of Ethiopia and were required to resettle mostly in Eritrea. In some parts of southern and western regions in the country, land was transferred to commercial farm contractors. The transformation has aggravated ethnic-conflicts and pushed people to resettle in the already densely populated settlement areas in the highland regions. Moreover, when the land redistribution proclamation was introduced in the Amhara Regional State in 1997 (FGE, 1997), thousands of discriminated farmers, who were classified as former government collaborators or "bureaucrats", became landless or remained with very small land-holdings. As observed by the author of this book, this land redistribution resulted in poor agricultural outputs and forced people to relocate in environmentally sensitive agro-ecological zones. Moreover, people who had no ownership rights to land, forests and wildlife exposed the biophysical environment to wanton destruction. As a result, people were pushed out from their original settlements by environmental hazards such as damaging floods and diseases.

In order to reshape the national economy of Ethiopia and to incorporate it into the global market, the present government introduced the free market economic policy in 1996. This policy, however, has not yet brought about the integration between urban and rural settlements (Wolday, 2000). Rather it has aggravated environmental degradation, which is associated with export-oriented agricultural crop production and rapid rural-urban migration leading to the concentration of a large number of poor people in the unprepared urban areas. In order to implement the new free market economic policy and the present resettlment programme effectively the following mechanisms need to be addressed effectively.

Since land is still in the hands of the State, which is not conducive to the effective implementation of the new economic policy, the farmers and industrial workers do not have the incentives to produce adequate food, export and consumer goods. Presently per capita ownership of land is very small and is decreasing. On the other hand despite the shortage of housing and lack of employment opportunities in the urban areas, rural-urban migration rates and squatter settlements are growing rapidly (Mengistu & Sjöberg, 1999). But through improved land ownership policy and sustainable agricultural technologies, effective trade links and communications between urban and rural areas could be possible. Such measures could encourage people to invest in the more labour intensive light industries, which absorb large numbers of labourers.

Massive imported goods have negatively affected the demand for the locally produced commodities. One of the most affected firms is the shoe factory. Some of the groups of people hit hardest by the new economic policy are artisans and blacksmiths. Self-trained traditional technologists collect discarded metal, glass-bottles, aerosol cans, plastic containers and the like, and convert them to valuable products which are highly needed both for the urban and rural dwellers. This could constitute an important cottage industry. Therefore, measures should be taken to encourage the development of traditional technologies. Among these are the following: (a) development of appropriate technology at the local, regional and national levels; (b) urban waste disposal methods of technologies; (c) adaptation of recycling scheme; and (d) alleviation of the shortage of industrial goods and foreign exchange.

The development of the small business communities both in the formal and informal sectors would serve as links between the farmers and the traditional technologists and producers and consumers. The importation of foreign industrial goods by big companies and corporations, high taxes, license restrictions and bureaucratic constraints has weakened the local business people. All these have in turn led to displacement and settlement-resettlement problems throughout the country.

The above-mentioned problems aggravated population pressure, shortage of land and environmental degradation. As a result, millions of people had faced serious food security problems. In order to promote food security, the post-1991 government introduced a new resettlement programme.

4.5 The New Resettlement Programme

Before the new programme was embarked, small-scale resettlement was practised. For instance, following the annexation of the fertile areas of Setit-Humera and Wolkayt in Gondar to the Tigray *Killil*, the Tigray Regional State resettled more than 14,000 Tigreans in Humera alone in 1993 and 1994. When over 14 million people were threatened with starvation in 2001/2002, the federal government of Ethiopia has launched a large-scale resettlement programme. The main objective of the new resettlement programme is to resettle about 2.2 million chronically food insecure peasants from the highland to the lowland regions. The programme is said to be based on voluntarism, intra-regional, self-reliance, community management, environmental concerns, and income and employment creation. It is larger than that undertaken by the previous socialist government. The estimated cost to resettle these people was about 140 million Birr (8.60 Eth.Bir = 1.00 USD). In the last two years alone, about 225,000 peasants were resettled in Amhara, Oromo and Tigray lowland regions as well as Southern Nation and Nationalities People's Region. The total cost was more than 121 million Birr (Ministry of Rural Development, 2003). The costs would have been more than that if the human and biophysical environmental costs were included.

As discussed in the previous and the coming chapters, well-formulated resettlement programmes alone have not solved the various problems facing the resettlement schemes in the country. Whether or not the new resettlement strategies are going to be implemented successfully, we need to know if the following basic questions are addressed before the programme was embarked.

- Is resettlement a solution to tackle food insecurity, extreme poverty and environmental degradation in the country?

- How much planners tried to look at other solution, such as increase agricultural productivity and alternative employment system through sustainable agricultural technology, urbanisation and industrialisation, rather than resettlement?
- People living in the highlands are always careful in avoiding living in the lowland regions due to the various diseases. Have planners provide settlers with better infrastructure such as housing, health clinics, wells, roads and schools before moving people to the new resettlement regions?
- The resettlement is said to be voluntary, but what does voluntary resettlement mean in the country where the majority of people live under extreme poverty, land, food and environmental insecurity as well as lack of geographical knowledge of the receiving regions?
- The newly resettled are confined to their own regions - intra-region. Is sufficient and productive land available? If so, is it possible to provide the necessary imputes and to produce variety of crops similar to the one in the sending regions? Are we sure that there will not be serious conflicts between the newly resettled and natural resources and among the different land-users?
- Do planners have the resources and experts to make the programme economically sustainable and environmentally viable; and do they take the necessary measures to avoid malnutrition and possible returnees from the resettlement areas?
- Did planners and policy-makers openly discuss with the population and persons from traditional institutions both in the receiving and sending regions about the establishment of the resettlement programme and its positive and negative effects on the receiving regions?
- Are business communities and national organisations convinced to participate in the resettlement programme?
- Are international financial institutions and donor countries willing to contribute to long-term financial package to the resettlement programme in the form of development aid and debt relief?

In order to answer the above-mentioned questions, detailed filed-based studies are required, which will be the future of a research agenda. With this in mind we now turn to the Summary of this Chapter, which Gambela as a Case Study Region will follow.

4.6 SUMMARY

In this section, an attempt has been made to examine the resettlement processes and their impact on the biophysical and human environments in Ethiopia. The previous resettlement processes occurred through both the southward and northward movements of people. The northward-southward movements of population are as old as the history of Ethiopia itself. These processes have produced both negative and positive results. On the positive side: (a) they have served as a survival strategy; and (b) they have played a key role in the development of the Ethiopian nation by accelerating the process of biophysical adaptation, cultural assimilation and integration. On the negative side: (a) the favourable environmental conditions attracted early human settlements, which led to rapid population increase and the depletion of soil nutrients; (b) neither technological progress and land management techniques nor family planning and alternative employment systems have developed. The biophysical degradation has basically led to the northward and southward resettlement processes.

This author is firmly convinced that unless nation-wide environmental rehabilitation measures are taken seriously considerable numbers of environmental refugees are likely to be created. This problem can neither be stopped by government decrees or by voluntary resettlement programme or by the use of force. For instance the 1975 Land Reform, the 1984 Resettlement Scheme and the 1985 Villagisation Programme and the present government's attempt at Regional Government Administration have not controlled the spread of spontaneous resettlements in the country. In consequence, the deterioration of the biophysical environment and the attendant resettlement processes has continued as before.

Environmental degradation in the original settlements has resulted from a number of problems such as poor settlement patterns, human and livestock population concentration on limited geographical areas/regions and lack of land-use planning. The interaction of these factors over a long period of time has had a deleterious effect on the ecological balance in the settlement areas. When ecological degradation worsened in the original settlements they became vulnerable to natural hazards such as recurrent drought, damaging floods, hunger and diseases. Consequently the original settlements produced little or no food, which caused the local people to move first to the nearby regions and gradually to long-distant resettlement sites. These are the main reasons why the Oromo pastoralists moved from their original settlements in the Rift Valley to the relatively wet areas in the western, eastern and northern regions.

In short, the conflict over land resources and the depletion of soil nutrients have both become the main push factors. Although government policies played an important role it was the push factors, which forced the previous and the present governments to move people from the densely populated and eroded highland regions to the less densely populated and relatively fertile regions between the 1960s, 1980s, 1990s and 2000s. It appears that these conditions are likely to continue in the future. Recent studies indicate that 18% of the highland regions of Tigray, Wello, Northern Shewa, Eastern Sidamo and parts of Bale and Harerge have been severely eroded. In the high erosivity areas in the western highland regions, including some parts of Wollega, the soil loss rates reach about 300 t/h/year. It is estimated that by the year 2010 environmental degradation could destroy the farmlands of about 10 million peasants, 60% of who live in the above-mentioned agro-ecological zones (Hurni, 1988, Aggrey-Mensah, 1988).

Drought and famine not only in the most famine-prone areas of the Tigray, Eastern Gondar and Wello, but also in the Rift Valley areas as well as in Shewa, Arsi, Illubabor, and Harare and Wollega regions have already affected millions of people.

Through (a) Environmental Impact Assessment; (b) township and village enterprise programmes; (c) family and land-use planning; (d) water and energy development, appropriate technology and environmental protection measures; (e) wildlife development; and (f) controlled rural-urban migration, sustainable resettlement patterns can be established.

Presently there are two problems, namely: the 1980s resettlement schemes were hurriedly designed and executed at the expense of the physical and human environments; and the 1990s regional polices have not been successfully implemented owing to the lack of proper allocation of resources, poor administrative system and lack of understanding of the potential land resources. The two governments paid little attention to the indigenous environmental protection practices. When the resettled abandoned their original settlements in the 1980s they lost their identity, assets, strengths and morals. Now the resettled are left alone. The previous and present governments seam failed to implement the environmental protection policies. Therefore, the restructuring of human settlements is urgently needed. Since the regional governments have not effectively assisted the displaced people, major problems such as mass poverty, environmental refugees, hunger, land-resources-based regional conflicts and worsening environmental degradation have resulted.

Through the implementation of the existing environmental policy, the natural ecosystem can be rehabilitated. More specifically the policy should focus on: (a) the provision of incentives to the local technologists and researchers; (b) encouraging technological and environmental education, animal welfare and capacity-building measures; (c) recognising land as private property; and (d) introducing land-use, settlement and family planning.

Lack of community participation had become one of the main causes for the failure of many projects in the past and now. This was one of the major reasons why the previous nation-wide land reform, resettlement, villagisation, aforestation and soil and water conservation programmes were not successfully implemented. Although a limited number of conservation programmes have been introduced in all the regional states, tangible results have not yet been documented. Even in Tigray Region, which enjoys a disproportionate share of all the investments in the northern part of the country, the outcomes have not been as expected. For example, Hanson (1998) contends that the Hizat Chebera Earth Dam constructed in 1993, 20 km outside Mekele, was not maintained properly by the village administrative committee which was responsible for the project. The main reasons are believed to be the following: (a) due to the lack of proper planning and the Dam attracted cattle from the adjacent settlement areas. Such cattle wasted the Dam water as well as trampling the nearby cultivated areas; (b) since the farmers do not own the land they are not eager to protect the Dam; (c) since the women are not represented on the Committee they are not interested in protecting the Dam; and (d) the regional authorities are not involved to maintain the Dam.

5 CHAPTER 5: CHARACTERISTICS OF SETTLEMENT AND RESETTLEMENT IN THE GAMBELA REGION

5.1 The Location and Areas of Gambela

Gambela is located at about 770 km southwest of Addis Ababa (see Figure 8), the capital of Ethiopia, covering 26,000 km^2. It is situated at the junction of the two geomorphological regions: the Ethiopian Highlands and the South Sudanese Plain. Mocha and Kefa regions in the east, Welega region in the north and the Sudan in the southwest border it.

The Gambela Region is divided into six sub-administrative zones, namely: Gambela (the regional capital), Itang, Jikawo, Akobo, Gog & Jor, and Abobo (Figure 8). In 2003, at the time of writing, these areas are also the principal administrative centres or towns of the Region. The Abobo administrative zone, which is the focus of this study, is divided into seven Peasant Associations (PAs), which constitute the lowest administrative units in the administrative structure of the country. Figure 9 indicates the boundaries of the PAs within the Abobo administrative zone.

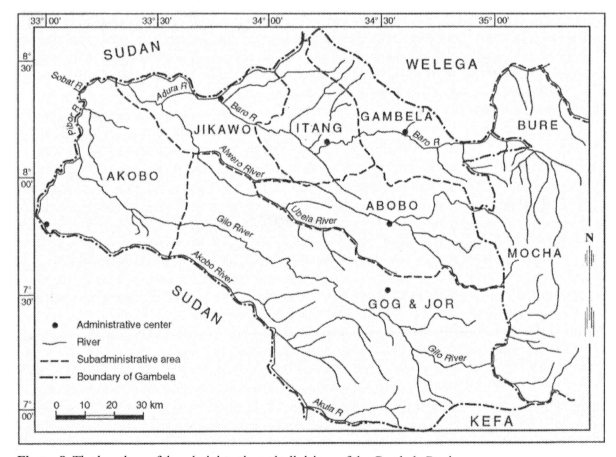

Figure 8. The locations of the administrative sub-divisions of the Gambela Region.

60

Source: This map was modified by the author from the from the topographic map (scale 1:750000, (Ethiopian Valley Development Study Authority, EVDSA, 1988)

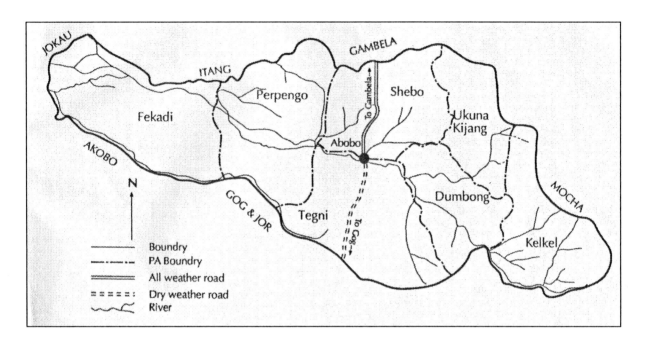

Figure 9. The locations of the Peasant Associations within Abobo (refer Figure 8).

Since the land with the best agricultural potential is located in Abobo most of the government projects such as the resettlement schemes and mechanised farms are concentrated in this area. Both Gambela and Abobo are located within the Baro-Akobo River Basin and have features in common. They share the same land forms, climate, precipitation and vegetation types. Hence, Gambela was chosen as the main area of investigation. Most of the soil, plant and other samples were taken from Perpengo, Chebo, Ukuna Kijang and the surroundings of Abobo area. Therefore, the findings based on the studies conducted in Abobo justifiably apply to the whole Gambela Region.

The reasons for selecting the Gambela Region are as follows:
- it was the second largest resettlement area in the country and is considered as representative of all the large-scale resettlement sites in the country in terms of structure and functions;
- the natural environment of this Region can be considered to be typical in terms of its richness in biodiversity;
- the Region is likely to be vulnerable to such incidences as flood, fire, drought and soil erosion if the present land-use pattern is allowed to accelerate;

- the region has hardly been investigated by serious researchers in the past especially from the point of view of its human and natural environments;
- until the 1980s the study area and its adjacent areas were more or less isolated from the rest of the country due to the lack of physical and social infrastructures and the prevalence of tropical diseases such as malaria and trypanosomiasis; and
- political and cultural factors.

5.2 The Biophysical Environment

5.2.1 Physiography

The Gambela People's National Regional State is one of the most remote lowland regions in the country. It is located between 33° 00' and 45° 30' longitude east and between 6° 30' and 8° 30' latitude north of the Equator. The Region can be sub-divided into the eastern, central and western parts or landscape.

The eastern landscape is situated between 1000 and 2000 m, and accounts for less than 10% of the total land surface. It borders the Mocha Mountains in the east, the Gore plateau and the Dembi-Dolo hilly and mountainous area in the north. The whole eastern part is made up of small escarpment and hilly landscape with sparse intermontane valleys and rolling relief. The land features of this part consist of rocky slope, intermittent and perennial streams, which have moderate volume and velocity. The land surface in the northern part is very dry while the south-eastern part receives adequate moisture. In view of the sizeable vegetation cover the streams and rivers do not appear to be exposed to riverbed erosion and some of the streams never reach the big rivers.

The landforms that are found at elevations between 500 and 900m cover the area around the Abobo and Gambela towns and extend up to Itang in the north and Uvela in the south up to the Akobo River.

The altitude of western landscape decreases from 500 to 400 along the Alwero, Baro, Gilo and Akobo rivers. The very flat and flooded topography of the extreme western part is characterised by swampy areas and gradually decreasing topography (i.e. from 400 to 300 m).

5.2.2 Climate

Most of the areas in the Gambela Regon are very wet for four months of the year and dry for the rest of the year. Mean annual precipitation is about 1100 mm varying from 800-900 mm along the western boundary with the Sudan to 1,350 mm at the Gambela town. The highest total precipitation occurred in 1978 (with 1497 mm) and the lowest occurred in 1986 (with 873 mm). The rainfall is evenly distributed but unpredictable (see Figures 10 and 11). The winds that blow from a south-westerly direction carry humid air from the South Atlantic Ocean while the monsoon winds blow from a north-western direction bring the precipitation during the main rainy season. The small rains between February and April are caused by winds coming from the Red Sea. August has the highest rainfall while the highest temperature occurs in April.

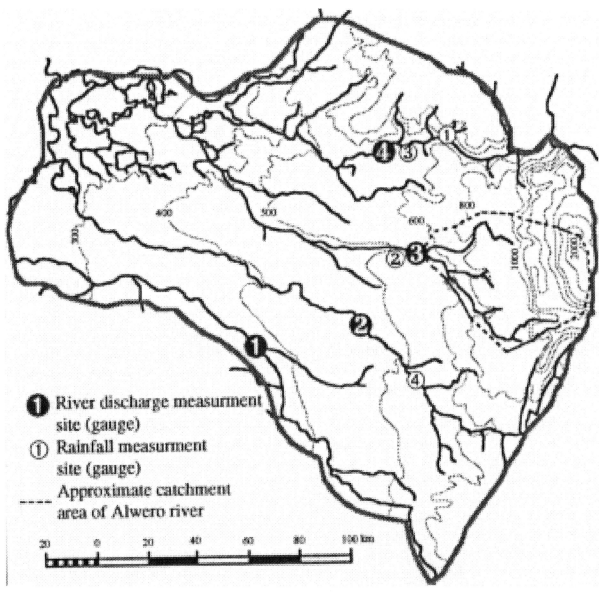

Figure 10. Map of Gambela: relief and contours with hydrometeorological stations.

Source: This map was drawn from the topographic map (scale 1:2 000 000, the Ethiopian Mapping Organisation, 1985).

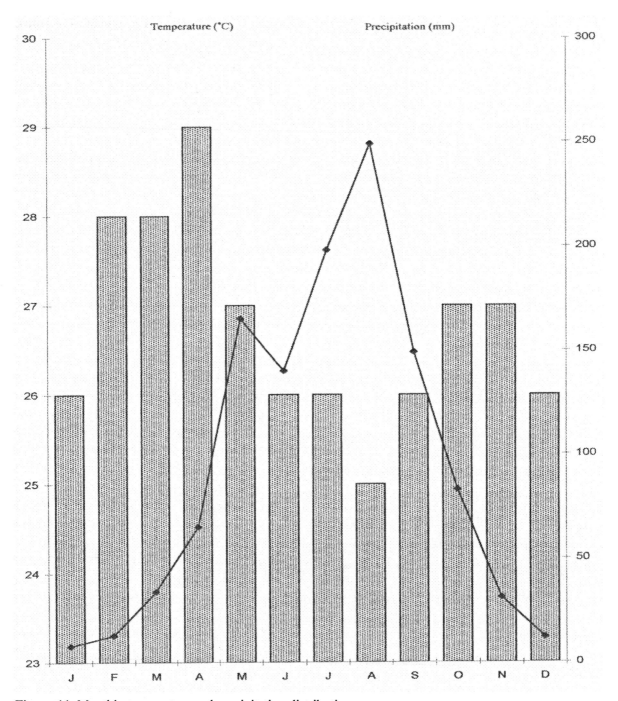

Figure 11. Monthly temperature and precipitation distribution

The Gambela Region is characterised by having a hot and humid tropical type climate (Griffiths, 1972). The mean monthly maximum and minimum temperatures found in the records were 37°C and 15°C respectively. The mean monthly annual evaporation was 1613 mm with most of the moisture losses occurring between December and April. The average wind velocity was as low as 1-2 m/s and the maximum 30 m/second. The monthly relative humidity was 74%. The highest humidity occurs between May and October and is lowest during the dry period that extends from December and April (EVDSA), 1990).

The main reason why the Region is one of the highest precipitation areas in the lowland climatic zone of Ethiopia is the fact that its geographical position favours high precipitation and high temperature levels. However, the forested and higher altitude areas of the eastern part of the Region receive relatively more rain (mean annual 1350-mm) and have lower temperature and evaporation levels. The western part has relatively low precipitation (mean annual 800-900 mm) and high temperature and evaporation levels. Owing to the dramatic altitudinal drop from the highland in the east onto the west, high floods occur in the rainy season.

5.3 The Human Environment

5.3.1 Settlement activities

Gambela is the Region in the country that was most affected by the 1984 Resettlement Scheme. Prior to 1984, only about 50,000 indigenous people, namely: The Anuaks, Nures and Majangers inhabited the Region, and the population density was less than 3 persons per km^2. Following the severe drought and famine that hit the highland regions in 1983/84, the previous socialist government of the country introduced a large-scale Resettlement Scheme and moved more than 600,000 people, especially from the malaria-free highland regions and resettled them mainly in the hot and disease-prone lowland zones. The Gambela (Illubabor) Region alone received 25% (150,000 persons, see Table earlier). Moreover, due to the civil war in southern Sudan at that time more than 300,000 refugees were resettled in the western part of the Gambela Region. As a result, by 1991, the population density had reached about 20 persons per km^2.

5.3.2 Land-use activities

The Anuaks, who are the majority, do not raise cattle but instead are engaged in slash-and-burn cultivation. The average landholding is less than 0.3 ha per household and the farming activities are carried out with rudimentary tools. In addition the people practise simple hunting, fishing, collecting and gathering activities. On the other hand the Nuer raises livestock while the Majangir are engaged in farming and collecting wild honey. Land in Gambela has been and still is under state-ownership with the indigenous people having only use rights. There were neither land disputes nor litigation. There were no large farms or clustered settlement patterns. Between 1984 and 1994, more than 140,000 ha of natural forest land was cleared for various purposes, but particularly the Resettlement Schemes and mechanised farms. Bulldozers cleared away trees and grasses for mechanised farming purposes. Such activities led to a high degree of environmental deterioration with increased incidences of flood, fire, and periodical drought and land degradation. This has greatly changed the biophysical and human landscape of the Gambela Region.

5.3.3 Social services

In the past, although the Gambela Region was nominally under the central administrative system of the previous successive governments, in effect it used to be administered by its own traditional leaders. Between 1975 and 1991 the then socialist government administered it and starting from 1991 it has been run by the present federal type of political system. In the pre-1984 period there were very few rural gravel or dust roads, and only one police station, a church, a hospital and an airstrip to serve the whole Region. After the launching of the Resettlement Scheme, the Region has been able to strengthen several government institutions. In addition, a new, relatively modern, airport has been built, the existing gravel roads have been improved and extended, new schools have been constructed, and trading institutions, health stations and shops have been established. Moreover, the Region's water supply capacity has been increased as well as that for energy with the introduction of an on-line supply from the main grid of the country.

5.4 Pre-and Post-Resettlement Administrative Systems and Settlement Patterns

5.4.1 The pre-resettlement administrative system and settlement patterns

In the past the Gambela Region was administered by its own traditional leaders. Between 1880 and 1934, Emperor Menelik of Ethiopia attempted to control the Region through his regional administrators who collected taxes for the central government. Dejazmach Jote, the governor of Welega, administered northern Baro; while Dejazmach Tessema Nadew, governor of Gore, administered southern Baro (Bahiru, 1970). After the Anglo Egyptian conquest of the Sudan, in May 1902 the British colonial government signed a treaty with Emperor Menelik concerning the delineation of the boundary between Ethiopia and the Sudan, the establishment of trade links with Ethiopia and the use of the Baro River as an important trade route.

In 1904, the first British trade centre was established at Itang, but was soon moved to the town of Gambela located between the Jejebe and Baro Rivers covering 400 hectares of land. The colonialists thought that Gambela town was a most important central place to: (a) link Khartoum with Baro for navigation purposes and to transport industrial commodities to Highland Ethiopia and export agricultural commodities to the Sudan; (b) attract the Ethiopian highland traders from the forested areas of Illubabor in order to extract rubber and export it to Britain via the Sudan; (c) control elephant hunting and profit from the sales of arms, ivory, coffee, cotton and the like; and (d) to establish coffee, tea, cotton and rubber plantations along the Baro River by hiring cheaply the Anuak and Nuer labourers.

Although the British benefited from the sales of arms, ivory, coffee, crocodile and leopard skins, among others, they did not succeed in implementing the plantation projects in order to extract rubber from the highland regions (Bahru, 1991) owing to regional conflicts between the Anuak resistance fighters and the new administrators. In order to reduce the tension, Menelik appointed a British officer;

Captain Bramley and Lej Iyasu appointed Yidlibe to administer Gambela and to collect tributes on their behalf. However, the new administrators were confronted not only by the Anuaks and Nuers but also by the governors of Kefa and Illubabor. The reason was that the central government: (a) did not send its armies to the malaria infested lowlands; instead it tried to solve the problems through diplomatic means; and (b) did not trust the Sudanese government and the British administration. Instead the central government sent Majid Abud, a Syrian Christian who had gained prominence in western Ethiopia, to the traditional leaders in Gambela asking them to submit peacefully. But after a few years of power struggle the resistance groups accepted the Ethiopian rule in 1932. When Italy invaded Ethiopia in 1935 the invaders administered the Gambela Region until 1941. In order to control the Region war broke out between the British and Italian armies which led to the deaths of many soldiers on both sides. When the war was over the administration of the Region reverted to the Ethiopian government but the British retained a presence there until 1935 (Bahru, 1990 & 1991).

Despite having the British, Italian and Ethiopian rulers in the region, the traditional political and administrative systems continued to be practised based on the village-structure until 1975 (Ellman, 1972 and Evens-Pritchard, 1972). Each village used to be administered by a village chief, known as Kwaaro, who used to be chosen from the dominant sub-clan. Under him there were always a number of deputies and a council of elders called Nyiya and Joa Dongga or Joburra respectively. A king called Geya ruled the whole region. Under him there were Nobles called Nybours. Under the Nobles were the Lwak and Kwai who were responsible for the socio-economic and political affairs of the villages. The Elders age-group advised the chief and the Geburs had the power either to accept or reject the king's decisions. The Gekugus were the spokesmen of the King.

However, the social hierarchies did not allow the traditional leaders to accumulate wealth. They had only social status, not economic benefits. According to the respondents interviewed during this study, both chiefs and the common people had obligations to participate in farming and social activities. Any political, economic and social matters were not decided by the chiefs alone; instead they were discussed widely at all levels of the community and then decisions were made. This meant that the traditional village-government system was based on a more democratic system than the system at the centre.

From the 1950s to 1975 the Ethiopian government used to appoint *Awaraja* (Sub-administrative region) and *Wereda* (district) governors and judges and formulate the policies and procedures, which they had to follow, but these did not substantially disrupt the traditional governance system. But following the 1975 Land Reform and the 1984 Resettlement Schemes, 35 PAs and a few Urban Deweller's Associations *(Kebeles)* were established (Figure 8) in the Baro Abol, Chebo, Perpengo, Ekuna Kijang and Ubala areas. The traditional leaders challenged the village and urban-based administration systems. The government solders killed some of the traditional leaders, while some others took refuge in the Sudan, and the remaining ones accepted the new system of administration of the Ethiopian government. But the new administrative system did not win the approval of the indigenous people due to the lack of an effective administrative system and financial constraints in the Region.

5.4.2 The resettlement administrative system

The Gambela Region *(Killil* 12) is one of the ethnic-based administrative regions, under the Federal Regional System. The latter is in turn subordinated to the Federal State Administration in Addis Ababa. When this study was made the PAs at village level and the Urban Dwellers' Association (UDAs) at the urban level were administering Gambela Region. Above these was the district or *Wereda* Administration at the *Wereda* level. All these are co-ordinated by the Regional Office at the regional level.

The indigenous people and the resettlers, residing both in the resettlement areas and in the urban areas, are members of the PAs and UDAs.

5.4.3 The traditional settlement patterns

There are two oral traditions regarding the origins of the indigenous people. The first oral tradition claims that the Anuaks originally came from West Africa and resettled spontaneously in the Sudan in the 15th century. From there they then migrated to the Gambela Region. The second oral source argues that the ancestors of the Anuaks descended from the Nilotic race (the Shilluk) of the Luo of Kenya and Uganda, and migrated up the Nile Valley from its source in Lake Victoria. Owing to the struggle for power and in response to the changing ecological conditions, the Anuaks broke away from the Luo kingdom and followed the White Nile, the Sobat, and the Pibor Rivers and resettled on the banks of the Rivers Akobo, Gilo, Baro, Alwero and their tributaries in the 18th century.

At the turn of the 19th century, the Nuers moved from the Sudan and resettled spontaneously in Anuak territory. The Majangirs came from a place called Inarea in southern Ethiopia. Most of them settled in Gudere outside Gambela town and a few others settled in over large areas at the edge of Mocha plateau. Linguistically, culturally and even in physical appearance these peoples resemble other minority groups such as the Tirma, Makan and Zilmance (Stauder, 1971). Presently the Anuaks are found scattered in Abobo, Jikawo, Itang, near Gambela town, Gog & Jor districts, between the Gilo and Akobo Rivers and along the bank of the Baro River (see Figure 12).

Biophysical factors shaped the settlement patterns. Most of the traditional settlements were located in the central part of the region with elevations ranging between 400 and 800 m as well as along the rivers and streams.

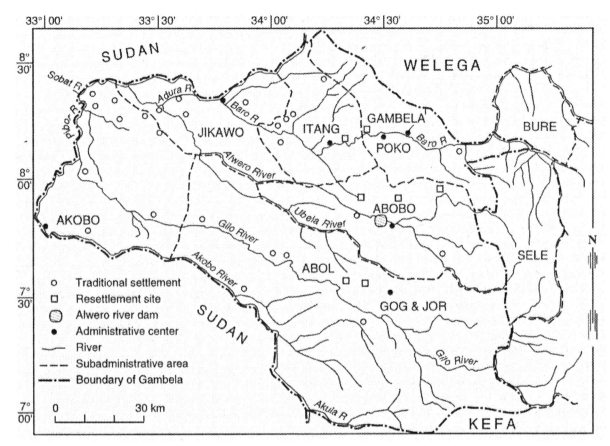

Figure 12. The traditional settlement and resettlement patterns

Note: A dote on the map is one settlement site or a traditional village consists of 1-10 huts and a circle is a resettlement site consists of 50-100 houses.
Source: This map was modified by the author from the topographic map (scale 1:750000, EVDSA, 1988)

The settlement patterns were associated with the different types of economic activities, such as agriculture, hunting and fishing. Most villages were grouped into a defensive unit offering protection against outsiders, and a grass fence known as a 'kal' screened a family house in the village. The land holding of each household in the different localities was small and was inseparable from the settlement sites (see Figure 13).

Figure 13. A typical Anuak hut

Note: Outside the huts are grain stores. In the garden, there are mango and papaya trees, sugar cane and sweet potatoes. These traditional food plants were potential to enable people to cope better with drought and without facing severe food shortages.

5.4.4 The socio-economic system and population change in the traditional settlement

The indigenous people lived in thatch huts, wore little clothing and slept on earthen-beds covered with the skins of wild animals. The women were responsible for performing the following tasks: raising children; gathering fire-wood, vegetables and root crops from the forests; fetching water from the rivers; going to the local markets; pounding food and preparing local drinks known as *borde* and *areki* made from maize and sorghum; as well as *tej made* from honey. The indigenous people practised a socialist-type socio-economic system. They shared their resources among themselves, ate and drank together and decisions were made on a democratic basis. If a person, for example, faced shortage in food he was entitled to receive assistance from his kinsmen or neighbours

The number of the total population in post-resettlement Gambela decreased owing to defection, death and abandonment. The number of the indigenous people, however, has always been constant mainly for the following reasons: (a) the tropical climate and water-borne diseases which are aggravated by the absence of medical facilities and nutritional deficiencies; (b) wars with other ethnic groups owing to territorial control, resource use and in-migration; (c) poor agricultural and food preservation systems which led to unbalanced food and seasonal hunger; and (d) late and restricted marriage arrangements. Traditionally marriage was not permitted before the age of 25 for males, and before the age of 18 for females, since the male was required to pay dowry *(demuge)* to his proposed wife and since most of them could not afford to pay, the number of married couples was declining. Few children were born since the women were overburdened with work.

5.5 The Influence of the Resettlement Schemes on the Traditional Settlement and Population Patterns

The total population of the Gambela Region increased from 50,000 in the pre-settlement period to 181,862 in the post-settlement period. The civil war in the Sudan drove 300,000 refugees into the Gambela Regions where they were resettled mainly in Itang and Fugnido in 1988 (UNHCR, 1988). By 1991, the number of refugees had gone up to 400,000, but in June of the same year most of the refugees had fled back to the Sudan owing to the political changes taking place in Ethiopia at that time (UNHCR, 1991). In July 1995 the number of refugees had reached 57,225. They resettled in Bonga, Fugindo and Dimma with their respective populations of 15,469, 31,704 and 10,052. In addition, a few people migrated from the highland areas and resettled spontaneously in the towns whose population increased from 9,000 in 1986 to more than 27,400 in 1994.

The town of Gambela expanded rapidly for the following reasons: (a) in-migration from the indigenous settlement areas and the surrounding regions; (b) the establishment of resettlement schemes and several government institutions; and (c) the new regional economic policy which provided new incentives to the possible investors in such activities as mechanised farming and various businesses.

5.6 Constraints Encountered by the Resettlers

The resettlement schemes or programmes encountered numerous constraints and problems. Among these were the following: forced resettlement; unplanned resettlement processes; concentrated location of farmers in the same ecological zone; distant water-supply points; long physical distances separating the resettlement sites and the various local economic resource sites such as cropland and water-supply points; and high financial, material and human costs.

Through the mobilisation of university staff and students and the employees of the various government institutions and organisations about 1,440,000 people were generally forced to move out of the Administrative Regions of Wello, Tigray and South Shewa and were resettled in the Gambela Region. These people were forced out of the original settlement areas by drought and famines. In most cases the central government had assigned quotas to the sending administrative Regions. The quota system in this context means that the central government decided to resettle a fixed number of people from different regions under certain criteria for a limited period of time.

The other problem was the ethnic-based relocation of the resettlers after they had arrived in the Gambela Region. The resettlers were classified into five ethnic groups, namely: Tigres (31.3 percent).

Amharas (39 percent); Kembata-Hadyas (25.4 percent), Oromos (2.8 percent) and Walaytas (1.5 percent). During the relocation process in 1990 the average number of persons relocated in each site was 1,124. The ethnic composition of each resettlement site varied considerably from one resettlement site to another. For example, in village "No. eleven", 90 percent of the people had come from Tigray, in village "No. eighteen", 80 percent of the people had come from Kembata-Hadya and in each of the villages, numbered 18, 19, 23 and 24, nearly all types of ethnic groups were relocated.

This arrangement initially weakened to some extent the feeling of unity among the resettlers. But as time went on the mixture of the people across the village boundaries become uncontrollable. Eventually this situation in fact resulted in mixed marriages.

Lack of planning was another constraint, which confronted the resettlement program. The resettlement sites were chosen haphazardly by the central government without careful pre-planning based on the ecosystems of the new areas. As a result the resettlers were not able to cope with the high temperatures of the resettlement areas as well as the new types of food and houses. In other words the resettlers were not able to adapt easily to the new environment of the resettlement sites.

In order to minimise the natural risks and hazards such as floods, shortage of rainfall and crop diseases, the resettlers, while they were in their original settlements, used to spread out their farms as they wished in the different ecological zones. But this was not possible in the resettlement sites since they were instructed by the authorities to concentrate in clustered settlements more or less in the same ecological zone. Hence, they were not able to minimise the risks that were associated with the natural hazards.

The resettlers were used to having adequate water supply in their original settlements from such sources as springs, rivers and natural wells. But the water wells in the resettlement sites were not adequate as they normally dried up in the dry season. Moreover, most of the time the water-pumps were not functioning properly. As a consequence, the women travelled to distant places to fetch river-water, which was invariably infected with water-related diseases.

The other major problem is the long physical-distance separating the resettlement sites and the local economic resource sites such as cropland, water-supply points, grazing land fire-wood places, traditional market areas, all-weather roads and other service-providing centres like court-houses, police stations, churches and mosques.

In view of these problems or constraints, most of the resettlement sites had been abandoned in 1990s when this study was made. This development raises many soul-searching questions that ought to confront the policy-makers in the future.

6 CHAPTER 6: THE SOILS OF THE GAMBELA REGION

6.1 Research on the Soils of the Gambela Region

Not many serious works have been produced to date regarding the soils of the Gambela Region. One notable contribution in this respect is the soil survey conducted south of the Baro River by TAMS (1976). This survey covered about 66,500 ha. The National Soil Service Projects and Land-Use Planning and Regulatory Department in 1985 conducted a soil fertility evaluation of the Abobo Sub-Region. In this evaluation 92 soil samples were collected from traverses covering 39,000 hectares of land along the Abobo-Gambela road, 10 km north of Abobo town. The soil samples were examined regarding their texture, organic matter, total nitrogen, and availability of phosphorous and potassium. The soils were classified by EVDSA (1988) in 1986 and one regional site in Abobo (among the 11 trial sites in Gambela), covering 2,137 hectares, was studied in association with a regional soil fertility evaluation project. As a result, soil maps at scales of 1:750,000 and 1:200,000 were produced and subsequently revised by TAMS-ULG in 1996 (Figure 14).

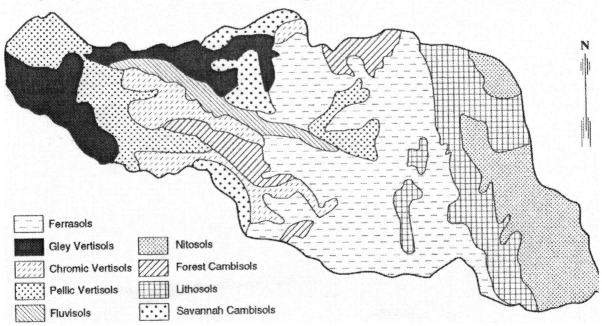

Figure 14. The soil types of Abobo

The formation, types, properties and spatial distribution of the soils are resulted from the geological and geomorphological features of the region (see also Appendix 1).

6.2 Effects of Resettlements on the Soil Resources

The results of analyses of soil properties in the different land-use types (forestland, grassland, traditional settlement and farmland, resettlement and mechanised farm) are presented here (Table 4). See also Mengistu et al., 2001.

Table 4. Soil properties in different land-uses

1	2	3	4	5	6	7	8	9	10	11	12	13
Forest land	18	39	43	CL,SL,SCL	4.0	2.9	0.82	86	348	1.86	1.03	0.19
Grass land	31	30	39	C,L,S.SiC	6.2	1.7	0.63	56	293	1.40	0.97	0.03
Traditional Settlement and farmland	30	41	30	C,CL,L,SiC, SiCL	6.9	3.6	0.25	109	423	2.86	1.16	0.08
Resettlement and farmland	33	26	41	C,L,S,SiC	6.1	2.1	0.11	32	186	2.00	1.09	0.06
Mechanised farmaland	48	22	25	C,L,SiC, SiCL	6.3	2.2	0.13	33	125	1.86	0.99	0.06

Note: 1. Land-use types; 2. Sand (%); 3. Silt (%); 4. Clay (%); 5. Classification; 6. pH; 7. Organic matter; 8. Total N (%); 9. Available P (as P_2O_5) (kg/ha); 10. Available K (as K_2O) (kg/ha); 11.Exchangable base meq (100 g soil)-[1] Ca; 12. Exchangeable base meq (100 g soil)-[1] Mg; 13. Exchangeable base meq (100 g soil)-[1] Na.

Classification: C= Clay; L= Loam; S= Sand; CL= Clay Loam; SCL= Sand Clay Loam; SL= Sand Loam; SiC= Silt Clay; SiCL= Silt Clay Loam.
Note. Average soil properties for each of the five different land-uses in Abobo. The data given in this table are calculated as a mean of the seven samples taken from each of the land-use type.
Source: Field data, 1991.

In western and northern Abobo, forests grow on sandy loam soils. In the central and northern Perpengo area, soil textures under forests vary from clay to clay loams. About 55% of the topsoils are loamy clay in western Dumbong, eastern Shebo and western Ukuno Kijang. In general, the forest soils in western Perpengo are deep and very dark while the topsoils are non-calcareous. The forest soils in Ukuna Kijang were developed over Nitosols with a good water holding capacity. The soils are derived from basalts, which are relatively well drained owing to the undulating slope. Since the forest soils are sandy loams and clay loams they have excellent porosity, good drainage, better moisture supply, lower soil temperatures and a higher level of biological activity than the grassland soils.

Clay soils are dominant in the grasslands, especially in Dumbong, Ukuna Kijang and Kelkel areas. The forest Cambisols are characteristically brownish comprising clay and loams, with a high humus content resulting from basalt weathering products and has a good water holding capacity. Soils close to the riverbank, particularly the fluvisols and ferralsols in southern Ukuna Kijang and northern Perpengo, are sandier in texture than in rain-fed farms around the traditional settlements. Soils in western Perpengo, where water logging occurs, are finer textured than the soils close to the riverbanks. The velocity and volume of the annual floods largely determine the size and amount of coarse sandy particles and the richness of the soils in nutrients.

Most of the indigenous settlements and farmland used to be located on the silty clay loam and clay loam soils. These soils were found in localised depressions and were very plastic and sticky when wet.

Under conditions of prolonged rainfall, the soils remain virtually saturated leading to severe water logging due to their poor physical properties and drainage. During the dry season these same soils become hard and crack, which creates problems for any type of cultivation. Soil organic matter was greatest in the traditional settlements and forested lands, moderate in the resettlement and mechanised farmland, and lowest in the grassland areas (Table 4). These findings contradict Birkland's report (1984), which suggests that organic matter may be higher in grassland than in forest because grassland receives organic material both from litter fall and root decay, whereas the forest land receives organic matter only from litter fall. Grasses in Abobo grow fast and when they dry, the above ground material is burnt either deliberately or as a result of wildfire. Therefore, the surface soils under Abobo grassland do not receive as much decayed materials as forested land. In contrast to the grassland, forest areas consist of different species of dense, small and large trees, and new shrub vegetation. Soils in the traditional settlements and hoe-cultivated farmlands contain more organic matter (average 3.6%) than soils in the resettlement sites - a clear indication of loss in the resettlement soils.

Resettlement and the mechanisation of agriculture have taken place mainly in the forest and grassland areas in the central and north-eastern parts of Abobo, between 474 and 600 m a.s.l. Consideration is therefore given to the conditions of cultivation and impacts of resettlements on the soils.

Resettlement farms are associated with tractor-based cultivation. Soils in these areas, and similarly in other mechanised State farms are more degraded than those under other types of land-use are. The negative impacts are associated with unplanned resettlement patterns, trampling of land by humans, tractor movement and free grazing activities during the wet season. During the dry season, the plant residue is cleared and burnt in order to prevent infestation by wild animals and insects, and for farming. In many areas over which fire has spread, the soils are profoundly degraded, and the ground surface is compacted by mechanisation. Thus tillage is more difficult in comparison to other land types.

The pH of surface soils in the forest areas is slightly acid (average 4). The soils are mostly derived from basalts, which are relatively well-drained with undulating slope. In the grassland areas, soil pH in the sandy soils were weakly acidic in all of the sites' samples. The pH values of soils in the traditional settlement and hoe-cultivated lands varied from slightly alkaline in the loamy soils to slightly acidic in the silty clays (average 6.9). This may indicate that these soils are leached to varying degrees, likely linked to the varying hydrological conditions of the traditional riverbank farm sites, due to high intensity of rainfall and deforestation related flooding. Soils in the resettlement and mechanised farms are more affected than those under other types of land-use. The pH values in the resettlement sites where soils are generally moderately acidic (pH 5.4 to 6.7; average 6.1). In the mechanised farmlands, soil pH varied from moderately acidic (pH 4.9 in the silty clay loam) to slightly alkaline (average pH 6.3) in the silty clays.

Total N (nitrogen) was greatest in the forest and grassland areas and lowest in the resettlement and mechanised farmland areas. The values of Total N in the traditional settlement areas are significantly different from the values recorded from each of the other land-use types. This may be attributed to the fact that land resources management in the other land-use types disturbs organic matter content and this in turn, reduces the values of N. The highest values of available P (phosphorus) and K (potassium) are found in the traditional settlement areas, while the lowest values are associated with soils in the resettlement and mechanised farmlands. Where soils are shallow in forested areas, the values of available P and K are low. Very high values of available P and K (up to 86 kg per ha P_2O_5 and 348 kg per ha K_2O) were found in grassland clay soils characterised by poor drainage, while available P and K values were consistently high in the river bank farm soils in the traditional settlement and farm sites. This is due to flood-related silty accumulation as well as sustainable plot management.

The soil nutrient status of the traditional hoe-cultivated land is generally high in comparison to the other types of land-use. The soils with silty clay loam and clay texture are more fertile than those with sandy clay loam and loam texture. Shifting-cultivation with rudimentary tools is practised in the traditionally settled areas and there are no problems associated with population pressure on the land or soil surface compaction. The low amounts of K under State mechanised farmland may result from surface and internal leaching processes as well as the lack of mulching and fallowing. Soil nutrients may also be lost through surface cracks in the clay-rich vertisols of the traditional cultivation areas. However, these traditional farm areas are better managed through long fallowing practices, crop rotation, the use of hoes, fire controlling techniques and mulching.

The tractor-based State and resettlement farmlands are much lower in available K and P, total N and organic matter than the traditional farmlands. This can be associated with a high nutrient removal in crops as compared to the traditional farming. As a result, resettlement and State farmland soils require fertilisation and a more sustainable use of land if adequate yields are to be maintained. The degraded nature of the land surface seems to have resulted in accelerated leaching of soil nutrients and lower values in comparison to other types of land-uses. Decreases in available K and P can be due to removal by crops, a lack of recycling of the nutrients and decreased potential of soils to fix P. Moreover, P is one of the elements most prone to mobilisation in tropical soils.

Although there are no previous data with which to compare the present results, it seems that the CEC (cation exchange capacity) of soils in Abobo is generally low. Since CEC is a function of organic matter, the destruction of forest and burning might have led to the decline of the essential elements. Exchangeable Na (sodium), Ca (calcium) and Mg (magnesium) are higher in the traditional settlement/farmland and lower in other land-use types. This trend seems to be linked to the forest clearing and burning activities in the latter and more sustainable land-use, including mulching and fallowing practices, in the former (Mengistu, 1998). Studies at the International Institute for Tropical Agriculture (Mulongoy & Merckx (1993) indicate that after many years of continued cropping, the tillage plots where digging sticks or hoe-cultivation was used showed significantly higher N, higher exchangeable Ca, Mn and K and higher pH than where mechanised farming or tractor-based methods are employed.

As summarized by Stromgaard (1988: 370), "the changes in CEC paralleled by a corresponding change in cations like Ca and Mg might be explained by the intimate relationship between CEC and organic matter content: burning might impair retention of cations if it destroys organic matter". This is noted especially in East Africa, British Solomon Islands and in the Lua forest fallow system of northern Thailand. In our study area, it is also suggested that crop residues and other mulching materials encourage biological activity in the soil, reduce run-off and foster higher soil infiltration rates. The exchangeable Na values showed that grassland values were significantly different from traditional settlement, resettlement and mechanised farmlands, while exchangeable Ca was significantly different between the traditional settlement farmlands and forest, grassland, resettlement and mechanised farmland areas. During the pre-resettlement era the Gambela Region was covered with thick forests, grassland and swamps, and was sparsely populated by the indigenous people. The Anuaks, for example, were originally engaged in slash and burn cultivation, combined with hunting fishing, collecting and gathering activities. There were neither large farms nor clustered settlements until the then socialist-oriented government of the country introduced the resettlement scheme.

So far, a comparison of soil nutrient status between the different land-use types has been made. Now we need to know how much of the soil nutrients have already been lost, and how much more will be removed in the coming years. The findings from 1991, therefore, are compared with the 1985 results, which are the only data available to be compared with the 1991 ones (Table 5).

The soils in the mechanised farmlands have lost about 24% of their organic matter, 30% of plant available P_2O_5 and 21% of plant available K_2O/ha between 1985 and 1991. Appreciable changes, however, are not found for pH and total N. Despite the short period (1985-1991) of ploughing, flat topography and the very low grazing activities, soil nutrients were lost. The following factors seem responsible for the losses. When the 1985 samples were taken, annual forest burning (caused by natural and human induced fires) was practised and ashes were returned to the natural system. While dense vegetation grows on these nutrient ashes, the soils regain their nutrients. When the 1991 samples were taken, the land was under newly harvested cotton crop (formerly forestland) and few nutrients were returned as ashes. These losses are compensated neither by artificial fertilisers nor by manure. The conversion of forestland into cotton crop increases leaching and runoff. High K losses may coincide with leaching due to high intensity rainfall on the exposed surface.

Table 5. Fertility gap between forestland and mechanised farm land

Types of land-use	pH	Organic matter (%)	Total N (%)	Available P (as P_2O_5) (kg/ha)	Available K (as K_2O) (kg/ha)
Forest land (1985)	6.4	2.9	0.14	47	159
Mechanised farmland (1991)	6.3	2.2	0.13	33	125
Change in parameters	-2%	-24%	-7%	-30%	-21%

Note: The Table indicates the wide fertility gap between the forestland and mechanised farmland. In 1985 the land was under forest and in 1991 the same land was under mechanised farming.

The soils in the resettlement areas, i.e. those in the mechanised farms, were more gravely affected than those under the other types of land-use. The unplanned resettlements; large population concentration in limited areas; tractor-based farming system; burning plant residues during the dry season to avoid obnoxious plants and insects, and free grazing activities during the wet season resulted in considerable negative impact of the soil resources of the region.

An example of the land that was affected in this manner was found in the north-eastern part of the Abobo area located at elevation ranging from 474 to 600 m. This land was originally covered with Ferralsols, Pellic Vertisols and Fluvisols. The ground surface became compacted by the mechanisation process and, therefore, and it was more difficult to till than the other types of land. The mechanised farmlands had much lower contents of potassium, phosphorous, total nitrogen and organic matter than the traditional farmlands and forestlands. This can be associated with high nutrient removal in crops as opposed to the traditional farming.

This suggests strongly that the soils found in the resettlement areas need considerable fertilisation and systems of sustainable land-use should be developed in crop-yields are to be maintained. The degraded land surface is accelerating the leaching of the soil nutrients such as potassium.

The fertility-gap between the traditional farmlands and the mechanised farms is much wider than that between the other types of farms. The mechanised farms have low fertility whereas high fertility and extensive land-use are observed in the traditional farmlands. This is largely attributed to the fact that land-use management in the mechanised farms disturbs the soil structure and depletes the soil nutrients more rapidly than in the other land-use types. Therefore, though annual burning of forests still persists generally, the traditional farmlands are much better in plant nutrients than the mechanised farms.

In general soil erosion or degradation is a grave problem that faces Ethiopia. As a result the country looses a tremendous amount of soil every year. The erosion losses of the top soils are largely due to the following main causes: (a) topographic vulnerability to soil erosion; (b) relatively high annual rainfall concentration, divided into two rainy seasons (i.e. June to September and March to April); (c) intensive crop production; (d) over- population; (e) overgrazing; (f) unplanned human settlement and resettlements; (g) lack of sustainable land-use systems; and (h) severe deforestation.

Nevertheless, the causes and consequences of soil losses vary greatly from one geographical region to another. In the study region the main types of erosion may be categorised into two, namely: nature-induced erosion; and human-induced erosion.

Nature-induced erosion can be defined as the wearing away of the land surface by natural agents such as water, wind velocity, temperature change and high erosive precipitation.

Human-induced erosion is the removal of soils due to human activities such as deforestation and mismanagement of the soil resources. Owing to this type of erosion those soils that are found especially in the mechanised farms and resettlement sites are eroded and carried away.

In the mechanised farms, in particular, burning has been performed since the launching of the resettlement schemes in 1985. In order to resettle the people bulldozers were used to cut down and burn trees and other vegetation types. Moreover, to prepare the farmland for the next crop the agricultural workers used to remove the regenerating bushes and grasses as well as crop residues and burn them any time during the dry season. It should be added at this juncture that the burning of the forests has meant the destruction of the carbon-absorbing plants and the release of carbon dioxide and methane into the atmosphere, which contributes to global warming. All these undoubtedly have a negative impact on soil nutrients, temperature, wildlife habitats, hydrological cycle and agricultural and human settlements in the region.

Thus rapid population increases and uncontrolled settlements and resettlements appear to have contributed considerably to the aggravation of soil erosion in the region.

6.3 SUMMARY

About 85 percent of the country's population, who had inhabited the highland areas for thousands of years, had avoided the lowland areas of the Gambela Region for the following reasons: (a) the disease epidemiological situation in the region was unfavourable for both human and cattle populations; (b) cultural difference and lack of awareness about the receiving region; (c) the intensity of push factors from the sending (highland) region was low; and (d) the physical and mental distance between the receiving and sending regions. In addition, (a) the available arable land was limited under the exist technology; (b) the soils, in the flood plains in particular, had the problem of water-logging while some other soils had acidic elements; and (c) some of the areas are prone to seasonal draught and unexpected floods.

Despite these hurdles facing the Gambela Region, however, due to population pressure, severe-land degradation and famine, thousands of the highlanders were forced by the government to move to the newly established resettlement schemes in the study region.

The extent of the deterioration of soil fertility in the resettlment schemes varied from the deterioration found in the other land-use types. The soils in the traditional settlement farms contained higher organic matter, clay content, phosphorous, potassium and total nitrogen than in the other land-use types. If the ongoing forest destruction (i.e. cutting down and burning), wood collection, charcoal making and the expansion of unplanned settlements and resettlements are allowed to continue unabated the soil resources of the region are bound to be eroded and lost irreversibly. In consequence, in order to avoid such an environmental disaster, conservation of biodiversity and appropriate land-use policy ought to be formulated and implemented before long.

Prior to the introduction of such sustainable soil management systems, however, it will be appropriate to provide environmental education to the inhabitants of the region focusing on the benefits that can be derived from the soil resources of the region. More specifically the inhabitants will be made to comprehend the runoff, the surface flows, the nutrient retention rates in time and space, and the estimation of the nutrient uptake by plants.

Although most of the former resettlement schemes have been abandoned since 1991, the number of the tractor-based commercial farms, formerly known as state farms and the urban population are increasing relatively rapidly in the Region. But the indigenous people are neither integrated into the development programs nor freed from the effects of the depletion of the soil resources, deforestation, land degradation and ethnic conflicts.

This author, therefore, recommends strongly that the new regional government launch a new biodiversity conservation strategy to counteract the further deterioration of the soil resources of the region.

7 CHAPTER 7: LAND-USE AND FARMING SYSTEMS IN PRE- AND POST-RESETTLEMENT GAMBELA

The 1975 Land Reform and the 1984 Resettlement Schemes changed the land use rights and some of the productive land was converted to resettlement and state farms. Following the change in government in 1991 most of the resettlement sites and state farms were abandoned and later given to individual contractors.

7.1 The Indigenous Farming Systems

Prior to the introduction of the Resettlement Schemes, all the indigenous people communally held land in the Gambela Region. Land disputes or litigations were unknown for the following reasons: (a) the land was more than adequate for the small population of the region; (b) the agricultural implements, such as hoes, made it difficult for a household to cultivate more than 0.3 ha of land; (c) the region was free from large-scale mechanised farms and most of the region was not suitable for grazing purposes (d) the local chiefs were not interested in holding large-sized farms; and (e) there were no physical infrastructures that required extensive land thus leading to land shortage.

Theoretically, land in the Gambela Region was considered as State property. But it was the local chiefs who operated the land with all the other people having usufructory rights land. For instance, any Anuak had the right of collecting wild fruits and root crops from the forests and fish from the rivers, streams, lakes, ponds and swamps. Similarly any one person could come from other areas or clans and settle down and share the land with the other groups of people.

After the introduction of the 1975 Land Reform and the 1984 Resettlement Schemes the military government abolished the traditional customary rights and institutions on the ground that they were "feudal" and "anti-revolutionary". In consequence, the State owned the land and some indigenous farm holdings were converted to mechanised farms, resettlement sites, and road and dam construction sites. Consequently, land-use conflicts or disputes arose among the indigenous people. These resulted in the following consequences: (a) some farmers abandoned their farms and moved to towns; (b) some obtained employment in the State Farms; (c) some became soldiers; and (d) others were engaged in trading activities. The total area under indigenous household holdings decreased from 441 ha in 1986 to 376 ha in 1990.

The indigenous people in the Gambela region practice the slash-and-burn cultivation method and use rudimentary tools. Although the soil suitability of the region is not known accurately, the soils are classified on the basis of sight, smell and touch in accordance with traditional knowledge. Traditional settlements and hoe-cultivated lands were associated with small, individually managed, household farm plots (average 0.3 ha at the time of the survey) in the forest and along the riverbank.

Under the indigenous landholding system, three types of farming are practised, namely: rain-fed farming; the riverbank farming; and the spring season farming.

Table 6. Planting and harvesting periods of traditional crops under the three farming systems

Types of farming systems	Crop types						
	Maize	Sorghum	Pumpkin	Sweet potato	Papaya	Mango	Wild fruit and roots
RAIN-FED							
Planting	May	May	May	Apil	May	(*)	(**)
Harvesting	August	August	August	Aug.-Dec.	Dec.-Feb.	Feb.-April	Dec.-April
RIVER-BANK							
Planting	Oct.	Oct.	•	•	•	•	•
Harvesting	Feb.	Feb.	•	•	•	Feb.	•
SPRING							
Planting	Feb.	•	•	•	•	•	•
Harvesting	March	•	•	•	•	•	•

Source: Fieldwork 1986, 1989 and 1991.
Note: • = none; *) Once a mango plant is planted, it lasts for generations; **) No one plants wild food plants. Wild fruit crops are harvested seasonally whereas wild root foods are collected throughout the year.

7.1.1   Rain fed farming

All the rain-fed plots are located in the forest settlement sites and are surrounded by trees and tall elephant grasses. Activities take place between May and August. The cleared forest or bush, grass or crop residues are burned in April and planting is performed in May. According to the respondents the ashes of the burned vegetation are essential for fertilising the soils and controlling weeds. The farmers sow the seeds when the ground is still wet. They dig the ground deeply with metal -tipped digging sticks and handfuls of seeds are scattered. If all the seeds germinate and grow transplanting is used to fill the empty spaces. The possible risks are minimised by the following means: (a) seeds can be prevented from early germination until the onset of the rainy season; (b) loss of seeds by birds, termites and other insects can be avoided; and (d) some seeds can survive the competition with weeds.

Weeds are one of the problems faced in the rain fed agriculture. Weeding has to be done three times before crops mature. This is because both crop and weed seeds germinate rapidly in view of: (a) availability of sufficient rainfall and warm temperature which accelerate plant growth; (b) spread of weed seeds over fields by wind and other agents, and (c) farmers leave the crop residues on the ground for mulching which protects the weed seeds from being damaged and finally enables them to survive.

If the plot has been recently converted from forest to cropland, it can be used for seven to ten years. Nevertheless, cropping in the forest-covered land is more difficult than on the riverbank and in spring farm areas because: (a) the indigenous farmers do not have improved tools to break the soils and begin cultivation; and (b) crops are damaged by wild animals.

7.1.2 The river-bank farming

Farming is carried out along the riverbanks after the flood season is over. Land preparation is completed during the dry-season and planting activities start in October and continue until February. Unlike in the other farming systems, topsoil lost to the river is replenished with new fertile soils, which have been transported by the annual flooding.

The main reasons why the river-bank farming system is important include: (a) the soils are rich in nutrients and are easily workable; (b) weeds are not a major problem; (c) farm plots are close to water and fish sources; and (d) wild fruits can be collected from the riverine vegetation even during the peak dry season.

7.1.3 The spring season farming

Activities of the spring season farming are carried out from February to March. This type of farming is dependent on two environmental situations: there is sufficient moisture retained in the recently dried out swampy land facilitates crop growth; and, due to the hot climate there is high evapotranspiration increases so the crops grow fast. Crop growing is further encouraged by the small rains, which often come after February. Plots are prepared through the burning of grasses and bushes in January and seeds are sown in February. As the major problems in this farming system are the breaking of the surface and the dense vegetation, it is difficult to conduct large-scale crop cultivation under these conditions.

The degree of farming intensity may be divided into the most intensive and the least intensive types. The most intensive type is found along the main rivers while the least intensive type is found along the small streams and areas with infertile soils. Although the forest soils are not as fertile as the alluvial soils located along the rivers high agricultural productivity is nevertheless possible with the shifting cultivation system.

Although the three traditional farming systems differ in time and space, all of them are suitable for crop farming. The major crops grown include: maize sorghum; and supplementary crops such as mango, papaya, semi-wild fruits e.g. *Cordia* and root-crops, e.g. sweet potatoes, as well as legumes. Maize and Sorghum are tall and can compete with weeds successfully. They are also suitable for inter-cropping with other crops. Maize seeds are not easily accessible to birds as they are covered by a sheath; but sorghum is vulnerable to bird attack and both crops can also be damaged by wild animals, particularly elephants and wild pigs.

It must be pointed here that the tillage employed by the indigenous people plays a significant role in sustaining the environment. As was argued by Rothrock (1992), tillage can help to conserve the environmental system when plant residues cover the soil after planting and harvesting. These improve the biophysical factors, such as soil-water aeration, compaction, porosity, temperature, and plant-soil relations. These relationships can also improve soil micro-climate; plant-rooting zone depth, and soil physical, chemical and micro-biological conditions throughout the soil profile and reduce plant diseases.

Even though the indigenous people encounter occasional food shortages, such as between the planting and harvesting periods, normally there was no food problem in the study area. Maize, millet porridge, fishes, wild animal and bird meat are among the main food items. Other nutritional food crops include nuts, water-lilies and certain types of grasses and root-crops. These are mainly consumed during food-shortage seasons.

However, it was impossible to quantify food production since the Anuaks did not use any type of measurement methods. Moreover, owing to lack of preservation methods some crops are wasted. For instance crops such as pumpkins, fruits, fishes, root-crops, and taro are not preserved. But the Anuaks have a better grain storage system than the Nuers and Mazangirs. Maize, for example, is stored in granaries built separately outside the residential huts.

Owing to the introduction of the resettlement schemes in the region the indigenous survival strategy has been disturbed. The use of some wild fruits has been abandoned and honey gathering and hunting activities have also been restricted. This was mainly caused by the peoples' displacement from their original settlements. This displacement made the original hunting and fishing areas inaccessible to the indigenous people who were moved to the new resettlement sites. Furthermore, the traditional control methods of natural enemies such as grasshoppers, baboons, monkeys, drought, floods and human diseases were not understood and broke down in the resettlements.

7.2 Farming in the Resettlement Areas

The resettlers to Gambella had three major land-tenure systems in their original settlements in the highlands, namely: communal-individual ownership; communal tribal-ownership and private ownership. The communal individual ownership was mainly found in the northern regions of the country; the communal individual ownership, tribal ownership and private ownership were mainly found in the northern, lowland and southern parts of the country (Mengistu, 1986). In general land in the original settlement regions was the basis of all-communal ties, personal identity, and security, source of sustenance, asset, prestige and capital. The farmers had access to farm plots in different soil regimes or types.

But after the 1975 Land Reform, land was nationalised with every peasant farmer residing in the rural areas having the right to use farm plots within the judicial boundary of his/her Peasant Association.But land in the resettlement areas, between 1984 and 1991, was collectively owned. The individual resettler had no right to sell, to lease, to exchange or to transfer land to other persons. Moreover, the sizes and the types of the land assigned for resettlement purposes and for farming activities were determined by the state. The farmers were not allowed to cultivate crops in the different soil types and agro-ecological zones of the region because of the following reasons: (a) the farmers' activities were confined to the resettlement farms and (b) the varieties of crops that were grown in the resettlers' original settlements could not be grown in the resettlement (receiving) sites.

The total resettlement holdings grew from 1,376 ha in 1986 to 8,550 ha in 1990. However, in 1991 the size of the cropland declined by more than 89 percent whereas the land under the cotton crop increased by 92 percent in comparison to the 1987 figures. The decline of the size of the cropland coincided with the change of government in the country in 1991. This was perhaps due to the abandonment of the resettlement sites, physical inability of the resettlers and inadequate government support for agricultural development in the region. See Table 7.

Table 7. Land-use and crop output of the three types of farms in Abobo, 1985-1991

FARM UNDER INDIGENOUS POPULATION	1985	1986	1987	1988	1989	1990	1991
Land size under cereal crop in ha	441	471	473	391	381	376	-
RESETTLEMENT FARM							
Land size under cereal crop (ha)	-	1376	9221	9344	8675	8550	1000
Cereal crop output (q)	-	2934	40038	62700	82150	56375	48000
Land size under cotton (ha)	-	-	316	121	179	4386	3812
Cotton crop output (q)	-	-	2080	1114	9910	6231	7500
STATE FARM							
Land size under cereal crop (ha)	1061	1301	3038	3374	-	-	-
Cereal crop output (q)	9218	18445	50710	42569	-	-	-
Land size under cotton crop (ha)	555	9898	100	189	4500	6500	8500
Cotton crop output (q)	44440	2264	589	3807	15267	11267	54643

Note = output from indigenous farming is not available; q (1 quintal) = 100 kg
Source: Calculated from the data of the Ministry of Agriculture in Gambela.

The large-scale farming system in the resettlement region was completely new to the re-settlers. The farms were ploughed with the state-owned tractors and the resettlers themselves only performed manual work. At the time of the survey, the farms were was run collectively. The working peasants contributed labour according to age, sex and other criteria. Group leaders were assigned to follow the activities of each resettler and register his/her contribution, on the basis of hours, to the collective work. Payment was made on the basis of a point-system. Points were accorded and calculated yearly in cash and converted to grain-shares. The average number of households under a group leader was 330.

The resettlers were not able to produce all the food they required. For example cereal crop output declined by almost 15 percent in 1991 compared to the 1990 output. As a result they had to rely on government food assistance. The main reasons for the decline of food production were the following: (a) the resettlement farms were capital intensive requiring tractors, but the tractors began to malfunction after 1991; (b) the resettlers had no experience in mechanised farming and had little incentive to work in the new farming environment; (c) the resettlers preferred private land ownership and the introduction of oxen-based technology; but this was not made possible; (d) the food-crop production did not succeed due to the unexpected floods, drought and insufficient inputs; and (e) instead of using the indigenous maize seeds, which were drought-resistant and high-yielding, the resettlers were required to use a new type of maize seeds brought from the highland ecological zones. In short, the resettlement farming system did not depend on the biophysical environmental system of the region. The food crop production, which consisted mostly of maize alone, was low in quantity. Moreover, maize was not suited to the food habits of the highland resettlers who were used to consuming other crops such as *teff*, barley, wheat, sorghum, chickpea and cow peas. Animal products like meat and milk were used as supplementary foods in the original settlements. But they were not available in the new resettlement areas.

7.3 The State farming system

At the expense of forests and other vegetation types, the area under State Farms increased to 3374 ha in 1988 compared to 1061 or 1301 ha in 1985. Like the resettlement farms the State Farms depended on rain and tractors. The 1988 cereal crop output increased to 42,569 q compared to 9.218 or 18,445 q in 1985 (see Table 7). After 1988, all the cereal crop production was replaced by cotton production. The conversion of the land to cotton production was based on the reason that the maize crop demanded more labour and had high-transport costs. However, it was later found that the cotton crop had less demand than the maize crop in the regional market. On account of this lack of market, huge piles of cotton were burnt down in 1989. See Figure 15.

Figure 15. A cotton pile before being burnt down (1991)

The cotton harvest was supposed to have been transported to the market areas in December but remained on the ground until the end of January owing to bureaucratic negligence and lack of transport. As a result, termites, wild animals and unexpected rains damaged the product. Moreover, although 600 labourers were employed during the peak season the cotton harvest was not saved for the following reasons: (a) high temperature and poor housing conditions; (b) lack of adequate food; (c) water-related diseases such as malaria and dysentery; (d) underpayment (i.e. seven to ten US cents for carrying a bag of cotton); and (e) shortage of transport.

7.4 Farming Constraints

The main farming constraints encountered in the region comprise shortage of spare parts and maintenance for tractors and other large-scale machinery; wind-related problems; birds and other pest-related problems; and parasitic weeds and insects.

Because of the shortage of spare parts and lack of maintenance, many tractors and other farm machines (combines, trailers and disc-ploughs) were out of use. For instance, in 1994 out of the total of 166 farm machines, only 40 of them were functioning properly and this led to poor crop production.

Wind is one of the main causes of soil erosion in the Gambela Region. Wind has a negative impact on the crop plants before they reach maturity. In 1990, for example, winds destroyed 1000 hectares of crops, which belonged to the resettlements and State Farms. There were six main reasons for the destruction of this crop: (a) the trees were cleared away from the resettlement and state farms thus depriving crops of wind-breaks; (b) the planners and agricultural workers came mostly from outside the Region and had not understood the wind direction and the season(s) frequented by wind; and (c) although tractor farming worked the soils more than the traditional tillage, the loosened soil did not hold the plant roots strongly in place.

The Anuaks have been accustomed to protecting their crops from wind-related destruction through four traditional methods: (a) the plants around the crops were left unaffected; (b) they knew the time and directions of winds; (c) the crop species, especially the yellow maize, were wind-resistant and early-maturing; and (d) the seeds are placed in deep holes which helped the roots to grow deep in the soils.

The question is, therefore, why the resettlers and the state farm did not learn and use these simple but effective plant-protection methods. Three main reasons are provided to explain this. Firstly, the resettlement and state farms were designed on the socialist-based principles rather than on the biophysical reality of the region. Secondly, most of the program leaders, who were actively engaged in guiding the farming activities, were not sufficiently trained in the basics of agricultural and biological sciences. There was no exchange of ideas and experiences between the program leaders and the peasant farmers.

Among the major bird species that caused destruction to the crops were Cardinal Quelea, Red-billed Quelea, Weavers (Grasaa) and Red Bishop. The indigenous methods for bird control included: allowing small grasses to grow along the edges of the cropped lands; and mowing out elephant grasses and cutting down trees that served as bird-hideouts. Other crop pests included rodents, grasshoppers, leafhoppers, cutworms, crickets, army-worm, stalk borers, termites and green bugs that severely attacked the food crops leading to food shortage. There were also many weeds. The indigenous method of weed control is early and regular hand-pulling.

8 CHAPTER 8: EFFECTS OF RESETTLEMENT SCHEMES ON WATER RESOURCES

Water is an indispensable natural resource for living and non-living things and it is an integral part of the whole ecosystem (UN, 1995). Socio-economic development is impossible without the utilisation of water resources. However, population increase and the mismanagement of the existing water resources have forced water to be a limiting factor. For example, falling water tables, shrinking flows and depleting of aquifers and inland lakes have brought about negative effects on public health (Mayer, 1996). Unfortunately many countries, particularly those in Africa, have not yet recognised water as an economic commodity and therefore, still consider it as an unlimited resource. It is perhaps on account of this that they in general have not introduced water protection measures or well-recognised regional laws, which could protect regional water resources.

8.1 The Water Resources of Ethiopia

Ethiopia has great physiographic diversity with high rugged mountains, flat-topped plateaus, and deep gorges. The Ethiopian portion of the Great Rift Valley of Africa divides the two major highland areas of the country. The rainfall and river patterns follow the geomorphological features of the country. The major rivers, which originate in the highlands, have cut deep gorges reaching a depth of 1,000 m or more. Falls and rapids frequently interrupt their courses. Based on the hydrological division of the EVDSA (1§988), Ethiopia is divided into 12 major drainage basins. See Figure 16 and Table 8. See also Zewde, 1994.

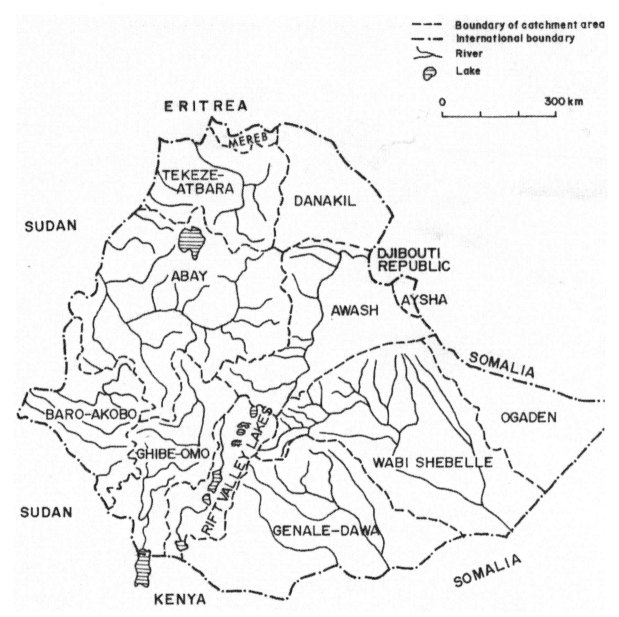

Figure 16. The major drainage basins of Ethiopia

Within the 12 major drainage basins are eight transboundary and one inland rivers and 12 major lakes covering 800,500 km². It is on account of this that the country is called the "water tower of Northeast Africa". Ironically, however, the country suffers frequently from recurrent drought and famine.

Table 8. Drainage basins, discharge rates, sediment loads and irrigable areas in Ethiopia

River basin	Basin area (km^2)	Runoff (10^9 m^3)	Sediment loads 10^6 m^3	Irrigable area (ha)
Awash[a]	112696	4.62	19	171600
Aysh	2233	n.a.[b]	n.a.	n.a.
Baro-Akobo	76102	11.81	10	734500
Blue Nile	201366	5262.00	40	997915
Danakil	74002	0.70	n.a.	300000
Genale-Dawa	171042	5.88	30	433300
Omo-Ghibe	78213	17.96	120	665320
Mereb	5900	0.22	1	9259
Ogaden	43692	n.a.	n.a.	n.a.
Rift-Valley Lakes[a]	52739	5.63	8	122300
Tekeze	82000	7.63	5	312700
Wabi-Shebele	202697	3.16	19	204000

Note: a Remain in the country.
　　　　b Data not available.
Source: Data from Hydrological Division of the EVDSA, 1988.

By and large, Ethiopia has not been able to divert its fresh water resources to the agricultural and human settlements and to construct hydroelectric power installations. It has also not been able to prevent its water resources from carrying away its precious topsoil across the national boundaries. Water-related fertile soil losses in the highlands are estimated to be 1000 million cubic metres annually (Jahnke, 1983) and the decline in grain yields, range from 0.7 to 1.3 tonnes per year (Hawanda, 1989). In view of these grave problems, Ethiopia has been receiving food aid from the international community for many years now.

8.2 The Water Resources of the Gambela Region

The total water resources of the Gambela Region, calculated from a catchment area of 52,800 km^2, amounts to 22.6 x10^9 m^3 and the average annual run off is 78,557.6 million m^3. The annual water losses, calculated from a catchment area of 124,000 km^2 are estimated to be 28.1x10^9 m^3. For further details, see the methodology section, Table 9 and Mengistu, 1999.

Table 9. A summary of hydrological data in major rivers in Gambela

Mean Annual Temperature (°C)	Mean precipitation (mm)	Evaporation (mm)	Water Resources $(10^9 \, m^3)$	Mean annual water losses $(10^9 \, m^3)$	Mean annual runoff $(10^6 \, m^3)$	Mean Annual Discharge $(m^3 s^{-1})$	Total HEP potential $(10^9 \, kwh \, y^{-1})$	Mean annual sediment $(10^6 \, t)$
27.8	1290	1603	22.6	28.1	78557.6	2489.2	48.1	14.921

Of the total annual runoff, about 80 percent occur during the high rainfall period of May to October, while 20.percent occurs during the low rainfall period of February to March.

The Baro-Akobo River Basin of Gambela Region is rich in hydroelectric potential, which is estimated to be 48.1 x 10^0 kWh per year. Compare this with the country's total hydroelectric potential of 67.4 milliard kWh per year (EVDSA, 1988 and 1990). The Gambela Region is second to the Blue Nile in its hydropower potential, but there is not yet a single power plant installed in the region.

The huge water resources potential of the region is, therefore, suitable for large-scale crop production with 738,400 ha of land identified as suitable for irrigation.

Although there is a dense vegetation cover, the mean annual sediment runoff is estimated to reach 14,221 million tonnes (EVDSA, 1990). However, there are no irrigated farms at all in the entire region. The only earth-fill dam is that on the Alwero River Dam, which has a full-reservoir capacity of 74.6 x $10^6 \, m^3$. The water from this dam was not being utilised in 2002.

Water in the Gambela Region is mainly from the Baro, Alwero, Gilo and Akobo Rivers and the tributaries of the Pibor River (which becomes the Sobat), itself one of the tributaries of the White Nile. These river systems are part of the hydrological regimes of the Sobat Sudd Swamp. The Sobat is one of the four sub-basins of the Nile hydrological system each of which have different physical, climatic and hydrological characteristics. The Sobat receives the discharges of the Baro (from the temperate Ethiopian plateau) and semi-arid areas, significant amounts of the annual inflow are lost through evaporation and transportation (Barbour, 1961, Conway et al., 1996).

The rivers in the Gambela Region originate at elevations ranging from 1,200 to 2,300 m in the highlands, drain as meandering rivers and enter the flood plains in the western part of the region. On account of the topographical and erosional characteristics of the areas the rivers create numerous shallow lakes, channels, ox-bow lakes and point bars.

The topographical and hydrological features of the region have produced permanent; temporary and non-swamping land surfaces as well as vast water-logged areas. The permanently swamped land surface is found in the extreme western part of the region along the borders of Jikawo, Akobo and Itang. It is covered with water throughout the year and has formed a marshland surface. The temporary swamped land surface is situated along the Alwero River and expands into the lower part of the Abobo Plain. It is under water for part of the year. Non-swamped land is characterised by sandy and loamy soils and is found at relatively higher altitudes. This large area has no standing water except a few ponds.

When a river reaches the lowest topography (inundated areas) in western Gambela, there is a backflow of water owing to the influence of the Pibor and Sobat Rivers. The hydrological explanations for the backwater flows include:

- all the rivers in the Gambela plain drain slowly in the same direction;
- the sediment materials carried by the rivers are deposited on the flat land and this hinders some water from passing beyond the plain;
- when the surface water increases in the Pibor-Sobat drainage system it pushes against the surface water from the Baro, Akobo, Gilo and Alwero Rivers making it overflow into the western and central parts of the Gambela Region;
- dense vegetation and water-logged topographical features together with the low water velocity allows the water to remain on the surface; and
- there is no internal drainage through the soil because impermeable materials cement the land surface and compacted heavy clay soils; percolation or infiltration is also low.

Heavy floods affected Gambela in 1988, 1989 and 1996. Table 10 shows runoff and rainfall data for the 1978-89 period, during which the mean annual maximum runoff was 689 x 10^6 m^3 in 1988 and the minimum was 441 x 10^6 m^3 in 1982. The depth of runoff also varied from 158 mm in 1982 to 247 mm in 1988. Although there has been no significant increase in rainfall in the post-resettlement period, compared to the pre-resettlement period, runoff coefficients are generally higher (Table10 and Figure 17), with the five-year moving average showing a gradually rising trend since 1984. This suggests that land-use and land cover in the catchment area have been seriously disturbed, resulting in the same amount of rainfall generating an increased runoff.

Table 10. Annual rainfall and runoff statistics for Alwero River at Abobo

Year	Rainfall (mm)	Runoff (10^6 m^3)	Runoff depth (mm)	Runoff coefficient
1978	1221	627	225	0.184
1979	946	476	171	0.180
1980	1105	521	187	0.169
1981	1333	541	194	0.145
1982	1125	441	158	0.141
1983	851	517	185	0.218
1984	1100	515	185	0.168
1985	1293	580	208	0.161
1986	778	565	203	0.260
1987	1081	556	199	0.184
1988	1382	689	247	0.179
1989	1075	611	219	0.204

Note: Alwero is the smaller river in comparison to Baro, Gilo and Akobo Rivers.
Source: Unpublished data from the Gambela Meteorological Station.

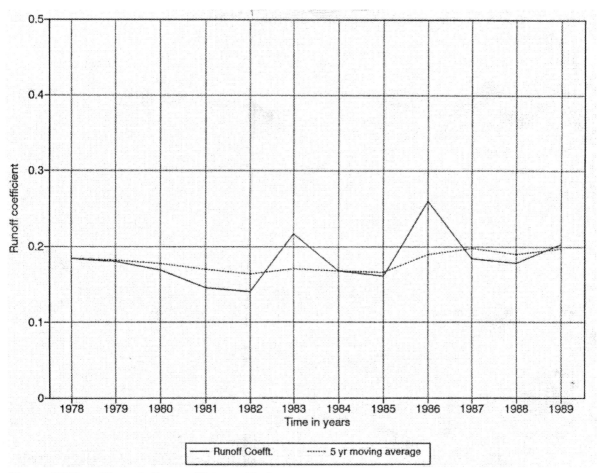

Figure 17. Runoff correlation coefficient with time

Source: Field work, 1991

Even though little is known about the sediment discharge to the Alwero River, the mean annual amount of the suspended materials is estimated at 200 g/m^3 and the mean annual sediment discharge at 0.12 (suspended load) and 0.05 (bed load) million tonnes/m^3. The sediment discharge appears to be small compared to the amounts recorded elsewhere in the country. The causes for this are low soil erosion, and dense and rapid vegetation growth along the rivers and streams. In the permanent and temporary swampy areas, grasses are tall and dense, and trees are scattered and shorter than those in the non-swampy areas are.

8.3 The Nature of Flooding, Causes and Effects of Flooding

Although large parts of Ethiopia suffer considerably from repeated periods of famine, there are also parts that experience heavy floods, often both in the same area. For example, floods from the Awash, Wabi Shebelle, Baro, Gilo, Omo, Megech, Dirma and Beshilo Rivers have brought about a considerable loss of human and animal lives, and damaged crops and property. Heavy floods have carried away enormous amounts of sediment from the highland regions. Following the 1984 resettlement schemes, heavy floods damaged crops, which had covered more 4,000 hectares of land.

Flooding that occurs during a normal rainy season is usually small and results from the morphology and drainage character of catchment areas, their vegetation cover, presence of a water storage surface, land-use and soil types. The 'normal' flooding occurs in many parts of the country. Such normal floods do not usually damage or disturb crops, vegetation cover, soil structure, plant and animal lives and human settlements, and are accepted as a normal process by the indigenous people. There are, however, abnormal floods that bring about considerable damage and destruction. In general both the normal and abnormal floods occur during the rainy seasons. The former happens seasonally while the latter takes place once every few years, particularly directly following severe drought. Farmers benefit from normal floods since they use them for growing crops. For instance, during the rainy season, water from the Baro River flows over a large area and remains there until the beginning of the dry season when it recedes and the farmers plant crops along the riverbanks. Flooding, in short, as a normal environmental cycle is indispensable for crop production in the Gambela Region.

Flooding in the post-resettlement Gambela Region has been different in that it has been largely of the abnormal type. There are five main causes of this abnormal flooding, namely: (a) excess overflow of the riverbank; (b) higher than usual rainfall and poor drainage; (c) lack of proper land-use planning; (d) improper utilisation of water; and (e) rapid population increase.

This author is firmly convinced that the abnormal floods have serious negative impacts on the human settlements and agricultural fields of the region. The abnormal floods come about as a result of the land-use changes consisting of rapid deforestation for the establishment of large-scale farms, and the establishment of several resettlement sites on the flood-vulnerable areas. Clark (1987: 67) contends that the forest cover reduces the river discharge "through the interception of rainfall and the evaporation of water from the tree canopy" and through the increased "hydraulic conductivity of the soil as a result of tree roots and soil organisms breaking up the soil". However, "Annual rainfall total is not sufficient to justify the conclusion that differences in river discharge are entirely due to the land use change that has taken place." Rather the main causes are faulty land-management practices and unwise government programs which all havens flood-aggravating effect.

The relationship between flood damage and changes in land use has been known for many hundreds of years. As Klein argued deforestation in the Alpine River region in France led to the destruction of properties by floods in the 19th century but when the same area was planted in the 1890s flood decreased (cited by Clark, 1987). In the area where deforestation decreased it is observed that the river discharge decreased also (Clark, 1987). Runoff, which is generated by inappropriate land use and deforestation, causes soil erosion and this in turn exacerbates flooding (see Figure 18).

Figure 18. Abnormal flooding of the Baro River

The socialist government, without properly understanding the hydrological systems of the Gambela Region, introduced large-scale farms, and these led to rapid deforestation and improper land-use practices. As a result, floods have damaged crops and property in the Gambela Region. Deforestation and settlement activities along the main tributaries of the Baro River have had profound negative impacts on the Gambela plain.

The abnormal floods in the Gambela Region have resulted in the following:
- crops are damaged by abnormal floods and are also affected by unexpected periods of drought due to the absence of irrigation systems and traditional agricultural practices;
- because of flooding risks, the areas that have high agricultural potential along the rivers are abandoned, and, instead, involuntary resettlements take place in areas that are far from the rivers and the communities have a scarcity of drinking water;
- the people cannot fish between the months of June and October because the floods are too high and dangerous;
- floods limit farmers' movements and prevent them from getting in contact with the other settlement and resettlement sites; and

- the abnormal floods increase and make it possible for dangerous animals such as crocodiles to come to the resettlement sites. Moreover, the incidence of flood related diseases also affect the urban and rural settlers.

Abnormal high floods occurred in 1968, 1971 and 1978 but they did not cause significant damage in the region. The main reason for this was the fact that the indigenous people did not stay in their settlements along the riverbanks, but were able to move away from the floods, and they also did not plant flood-sensitive crops. In contrast, when floods occurred during the post-resettlement years of 1988, 1989 and 1993, a great deal of crops and property was damaged, and some resettlement sites in Itang, Uballa and Abobo were abandoned.

Owing to the high clay content of the soils, which make them less vulnerable to floods, and the local topography, the river-water is discharged onto a flat land surface and the flood is forced to move slowly. Although deforestation in some areas has already brought about repeated flooding problems, the dense and fast growing vegetation types such as grasses and shrubs can protect the soils from being eroded. As indicated earlier, the sediment loads of the Baro-Akobo River Basin are lighter than those of the Blue Nile River Basin. But the question is how long can this situation prevails. There is already the danger associated with the newly introduced plant species (e.g. *Azadirachta indica* L.), which does not appear to give good protection to the soils since it cannot substitute the natural or original vegetation types of the Gambela Region (Mengistu, 1995a).

Looking at the problem from the perspectives of topography and vegetation cover of the region flooding is not likely to cause great damage. Rather the major problem appears to rest or depend on land management and the utilisation of the water resources. Unless a deeper comprehension of the physical environment is gained even normal flooding can develop into abnormal floods. Otherwise if the present practices of deforestation and resettlement processes are allowed to continue unabated it is more than likely that colossal destruction of the physical environment will be a reality in the not-to-distant future.

Many parts of the Gambela Region are flood-prone. One such example is the Alwero River Dam Project, which is discussed in some detail hereunder. The construction of the Dam started in 1982 and was completed in 1997. This dam was built primarily for irrigating about 2000 ha of land. This land was cleared and prepared for planting cash crops, mainly cotton, and to resettle agricultural labourers. But, 2002 had started no irrigation activities.

The construction of the dam and the threat of flooding are likely to have the following overall impacts on the physical and human environments in Alwero:

- owing to the possibility of the reservoir overflowing, the nearby settlement and resettlement sites might be submerged and the rising water from the Dam could lead to massive floods which could disrupt the physical and social infrastructures of the entire region;
- if the amount of the reservoir water is reduced, sufficient water will not reach those areas that are below the Dam thus affecting the fish migration pattern;

- the rise and fall of the river determines the planting and harvesting activities. If flooding does not take place, the agricultural fields of the indigenous people will not receive fresh soils with fine texture that would enhance the crop moisture content; and
- the likelihood of excessive evaporation, seepage losses, heavy sediment loads, and salutation hazards whose consequences have not yet been investigated.

It is important to note that the hydraulic projects such as dams and irrigation facilities can reduce flood hazards if they are designed deliberately for that purpose. But in the Gambela Region, the resettlements in particular were exposed to flood hazards since there were no flood hazard reduction and recovery methods. As a consequence, severe flooding is likely to take place from time to time aggravated by the new infrastructural and land-use changes. Human-induced floods are likely to be more rapid and destructive than the normal ones.

8.4 SUMMARY

Ethiopia does not appear to be able to use its water resources properly and at sustainable rates. Nor has the country the capacity to prevent its rivers from eroding and carrying away the countries indispensable natural resources, particularly topsoil. This problem results from floods, which are associated with unsustainable land-use and water-resources developments. This problem can be solved, at least partly, by the proper utilisation of the tributary and Transboundary Rivers and nation-wide proper natural resources management practices. However adequate attention has not been given to the management of the water resources both from economic and environmental perspectives. In urban areas, water pollution and environmental degradation have caused adverse health conditions, but investments in wastewater treatment and disposal have been very poor.

In order to save human lives the conservation of natural resources particularly land and water, are crucial. If the country does not use its available water resources at sustainable rates the conservation costs will be enormous in the future. Therefore, serious resources conservation strategies are urgently needed. Such strategies can: (a) create a deeper understanding of the resources by the users; (b) reduce unexpected floods and drought; (c) embark upon new and promising water development prospects; and (d) change the map of the physical and cultural environments of the country.
Although the Gambela Region is rich in natural resources, they are unprotected from possible damage by abnormal floods since they require large investments.

The post-1991 Regional Government of the Gambela Region has a new land-grant policy which facilitates the distribution of land to possible investors. Whether or not this new policy is likely to result in increased abnormal floods and general environmental degradation in the country remains to be seen. But presently the new regional government has not yet studied the possible effects of the new land-grant policy.

It is hoped that reporting this study would contribute modestly to a better understanding of the nature of flooding so that sound rural and urban land-use plans can be prepared to suit various purposes. Moreover, the 1988/90 and 1999 Master Plans ought to be implemented seriously in order to control flooding and introduce workable conservation measures for the region's natural resources, particularly water, soil, land, and forests which would in turn create possibilities for launching and implementing food security and poverty-alleviation strategies.

9 CHAPTER 9: THE EFFECTS OF RESETTLEMENT SCHEMES ON VEGETATION: AN ETHNOBOTAINCAL APPROACH

9.1 The Physiognomy of Plants

The present author grouped the Gambela vegetations into six and the Abobo vegetation into five categories based on the physiognomic classification by Pichi-Sermolli (1957), TAMS (1976) and EVDSA (1988). See also Figure 19. The types of forest described here also agree as closely as possible with the types used by White (1993), Tesfaye (1996) and Friis (1990). Friis et al. (1982) identified the forest in Gog, along the Baro River, as semi-deciduous Guineo-Congolian. Selected trees, shrubs and tall grasses were also studied by Azene et al. (1983).

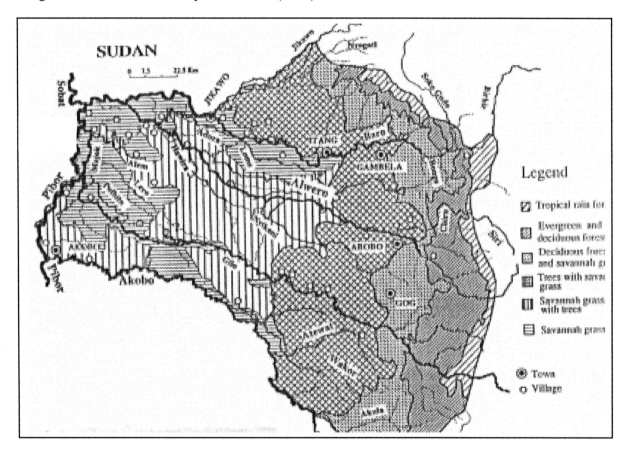

Figure 19 Geobotanical boundary of plant species in the Gambela Region

Note: Map of Gambela: spatial distribution of rivers and vegetations as well as settlement patterns. This map was designed and modified from the 1988 EVDSA's map, scale 1:750 000. Names with capital letters refer to regional administrative towns and names with small letters to rivers and streams.

The total area of the first geobotanical zone is located between altitudes 600 and 1000 m in the east of the Region. The characteristics of the plant cover vary from tropical rain forest and deciduous forest to trees with savannah grass. Between 450 and 600 m altitudes savannah grass with trees is found on the sloping and rolling plains; and deciduous lowland forests grow on the hilly-rolling plains on the eastern and south-eastern side. In the areas located at 550-m altitude, in the eastern part of the region, the montane evergreen forest and transitional lowland forests are dominant. Located, at altitudes between 450 m and the Sudanese border, on the western side, the plant cover is mainly savannah grass with scattered trees and riverine forest species. The evergreen tropical rain forest types are also found in the southern part of the region, approximately at the 400-m altitude level (see Figure 20). In short, the vegetation types can be classified into: (a) forests found in the eastern and south-eastern parts; (b) scattered trees; and (c) savannah (located in the central, eastern and south-western parts) geobotanical zones.

The mixed forests are found mainly in the eastern and southern parts while the deciduous forests are located in the central and south-western parts of the Region. Shrubs, perennial grasses and bushes mixed with big tree species are also widespread in the north and are found sporadically in the northwest parts of the region. The height of vegetation varies from 4 to 25 m and its canopy ranges from closed to almost-closed stratification.

Figure 20. The endangered evergreen forest in southern Abobo (1994)

The dense mixed forests are found mainly in the southern and central parts whereas the dense deciduous forests are spread throughout the study area. Within the latter type are plants which loose their leaves at the start of the dry season, while are others that loose their leaves at the end of the dry season. Most trees in the dry areas are deciduous and have irregular shapes, especially in the western and the central parts of the region. Montane deciduous evergreen forests and transitional lowland forests are dominant in the eastern part of the region at 550-m altitude. Savannah woodland is dominant in the west and central parts in the region.

Scattered trees and grasses are found along the rivers in the eastern part of the Region. The trees are found in association with grasses, and as scattered and isolated woodlands. The number of plant species in the geobotancial zone is less than in the dense forest areas. Limited areas in the southern, northern and western parts of the Region are characterised by dense forests while the deciduous forests are found scattered throughout the study area.

Pichi-Sermolli's classification of swampy land and savannah vegetation (e.g. *Andropogon, Heteropogon)* resembles the savannah vegetation in the Gambela Region. The EVDSA has classified the savannah vegetation types in this region into wet high-grass savannah, dry savannah herbage and savannah wood vegetation. In the swampy vegetation zone in western Gambela/Abobo grasses such as

Pennisetum purpureum and *Panicum maximum* Jacq. are dominant species followed by scattered trees (see Mengistu, 1995a).

Local knowledge and the authors' observations identify the frequent occurrences of fires as the most important factor in the formation of the Gambela savannah landscape. Prior to the launching of the 1984 Resettlement Programme, the Gambela/Abobo Region used to be inhabited by a large number of wildlife species. See Chapter 11. But following the arrival of the resettlers the original rich natural biodiversity of the Region began to be reduced appreciably by such causes as more deliberate fires and expansion of the slash-and-burn agricultural practices.

9.2 Forest Management Practices in the Indigenous Settlements

Very little is known as to how the plants or vegetation once disturbed will recover and the factors that could contribute to this recovery. The Model provided below has been built on from local knowledge about the vegetation and the author's long-term investigation in the area (See Figure 21).

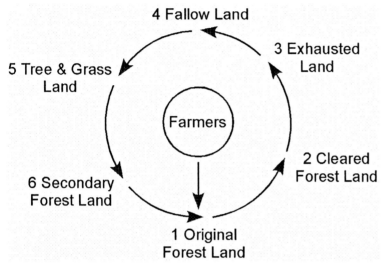

Figure 21. The land-use succession model

The land-use succession model suggests successive land-use types starting with the original forest, namely:

- the succession starts with clearing of the original forest land, which, after some years becomes exhausted owing to continued use;
- then it is either left fallow or permanently abandoned;
- this is followed by the stage when the land is allowed to rehabilitate itself through the natural re-generative process and becomes covered with grasses and trees;
- after a few years the land is covered with secondary forests where trees become the dominant vegetation type; and
- finally after about three decades the succession ends by going back to the original land-use type i.e. vegetation that resembles closely the original forest.

This model is applicable to the land-use pattern found in most parts of the Gambela Region. On the basis of the responses obtained from the indigenous people and through intensive discussions, the following six recovery conditions or mechanisms have been identified.

- The first recovery condition rests on the fact that the topography ought to be flat and soil should be clayey and loamy; the climate should be one, which is warm with high precipitation; and adequate water needs to be available for plant growth.
- The second recovery condition consists of the availability of carefully selected agricultural plots. Each household chooses a tiny productive plot from the forestlands. Only the branches of the trees

that have grown on the plots of land are allowed to be cut-down and burnt. The vegetation that surrounds the plots is not cleared.

- The third recovery condition requires time needed for the regeneration of vegetation. After the land has been used extensively for five to seven years the plots of land are abandoned owing to exhaustion and the households move elsewhere.
- The fourth recovery condition entails the absence of domestic animals in most areas of the Region as well as the presence of very few wild animals. Moreover, the population density of one person per km^2 is extremely low; and the cropland per household is also very small i.e. 0.3 hectare per household. In addition the resettlement sites ought to be widely spread. These conditions have not created any grave environmental stress in the Region.
- Owing to the absence of external interference exotic species, which would have affected negatively the recovery of the vegetation, have not been introduced in the region before the 1984 Resettlement Programme. It appears that that those plant species that have survived the disturbances must have contributed to re-vegetation thus leading to vegetation recovery.
- The sixth recovery condition is the fact that the Anuaks had abandoned their farms permanently because of the following reasons: (a) need for cultivable land elsewhere, (b) degradation of the soil nutrients due to negative consequences of the environmental changes; (c) high rainfall and temperature; (d) the protection of the landscape by hills and mountains from wind; and (e) poor physical and social infrastructures.

The prevailing difficult physical and human environmental factors drove the indigenous people to abandoned their areas and these were re-vegetated with secondary forests. However, unlike in the original forest, the trees in the secondary forests are short and are interspersed with different types of tall grass species. The farmers tend to remove the trees but allow the grasses to grow.

What should be noted here carefully, however, is the finding that the slash-and-burn cultivation method does not necessarily have negative impact on the natural environment. In fact, in the Gambela landscape this method appears to have a positive impact on the biophysical environment since it prevents the soil from being exposed to erosion.

Normally, the farmers do not cultivate former cropland areas since they think they would encounter excessive weeding problems. The indigenous farmers take many years to leave their colonised plots and open up new ones. After the harvest has been removed, the traditional plots are left unused for a number of years and are not exposed to soil erosion agents since they are covered with crop residues. Moreover, the traditional hoes do not disturb the soil structure. The crop seeds grow fast and with little rainfall cover the ground rapidly.

The land-use succession model is useful to understand as to how the system functions. This approach or model may also be used by researchers who are engaged in the study of the deforestation problems in the highland areas of the country.

9.3 The Post-Resettlement Deforestation Process

The term deforestation signifies vegetation destruction, which may lead to both biochemical changes in the soil as well as increased erosion (Hosier, 1988:123). It was estimated that 11.3 million hectares of tropical forests were destroyed per year in period between 1981 and 1983 (FAO, 1986).

Deforestation presents a serious threat for local environments as well as being part of regional and global environmental problems. As Hosier (1988:122) argued, "deforestation would represent both environmental destruction and economic problems. The only logical choice would be to halt it everywhere". Fearnside (1986) estimated that 20×10^3 km^2 of rainforests in Brazil were destroyed in 1978 and it is forecast that within forty years the rainforests will be practically eliminated. The situation in the former Zaire is far worse than the one in Brazil (cited by Clarke, 1987). Potter et al. reported in 1975 that the amount of rainfall fell by 223 mm and temperature surely increased by about 0.4^o C in the Tropics (cited by Clark in 1987). Through this deforestation process drought will not be confined to the local level but will spread to regional and global levels. This is bound to result in low biomass and agricultural output (cited by Clark, 1987). The main causes of forest destruction, especially in Sub-Saharan Africa, range from slash-and-burn cultivation and fire-wood collection to commercial farming and human resettlement schemes. It can be argued that the misuse of natural resources is partly due to lack of adequate information about the values of plant species and partly because most governments give little attention to research and its applications.

The losses of Ethiopian forests are not brought about only by the lack of research and proper management but are also due to the lack of land-use policy. Historical estimates suggest that the forest cover in Ethiopia declined from an original 35% to 16% by 1952; to 3.6% by 1980; to 2.7% by 1987 and to 2.4% in 1990 (Sayer et al. (eds), 1992). Although the previous socialist government of Ethiopia had introduced nation-wide afforestation programmes starting from the 1970s, the deforestation process was aggravated through the post-1984 resettlement programmes and then by the 1991 government change. The resettlement programmes were launched without taking into consideration the types of plants, soil properties, hydrology and socio-economic conditions of the regions affected. The Gambela Region has suffered from this problem as most of its valuable tree and grass species have been damaged due to the resettlement schemes.

Figure 22 shows that about 99% of the Gambela landscape had dense vegetation cover until 1984 when the resettlement programmes changed the landscape considerably. The numerical change is also manifested in Table 11 where the pre-and post-resettlement situations are compared.

The land-use/land-cover change in the post-1984 period is based on 1986 SPOT satellite images and 1982 topographic maps. To investigate the changes between the pre-and post-resettlement, 4 land-use/land-cover categories were distinguished from the two sample areas (C Abobo and NW Abobo): forestland, scattered trees and grassland, cultivated and settlement land and others. As shown in Table 11, there was a dramatic fall of forest cover from more than 80% before 1984 to 65% in 1986; with a matching increase in cultivated and settlement land from less than 5% in 1984 to more than 30% in 1986. On the other hand the area occupied by the scattered trees and grassland increased considerably in central Abobo but decreased in NW part of the region.

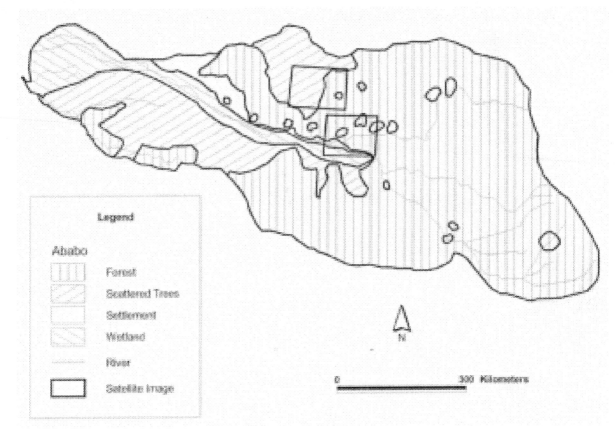

Figure 22. Land-use/land-cover of Abobo

Table 11. Land-use change before and after the resettlement schemes in Abobo

Land-Use Types	Pre-Resettlement, 1985		Post-Resettlement, 1986		Change in
C. Abobo	Area in ha	%	Area in ha	%	parameter, %
Forest Land	7558	84.9	1687	19	-65.9
Scattered tree and grass land	880	9.9	3637	40.9	31
Cultivated and settlement land	440	4.9	2656	29.9	25
Others	16	0.3	914	10.3	10
Total	8894	100	8894	100	
NW Abobo					
Forest Land	5140	50.9	3861	38.2	-12.7
Scattered tree and grass land	4940	48	3011	29.8	-18.2
Cultivated and settlement land	11	0.9	3208	31.7	30.8
Others	9	0.2	20	0.3	0.1
Total	10100	100	10100	100	

Note: Land covers category:
* Forest land: areas covered by dense trees forming closed canopy.
* Scattered tree and grassland: land covered by sparse trees and dense grass. Grasses are dominated by *Pennisetum purpureum.*
* Cultivated land: areas covered by tractor-based cotton and maize crops.
* Other land: land occupied by water body, huts, offices, storage, warehouse, etc.
* Settlement: all types of settlements

Based on the fieldwork by the author in the 1990s, deforestation activities were not only confined to the resettlement areas in Abobo but also spread throughout the Gambela Region. Much of the vegetation cover was cleared and burned to give way to farmland, grazing and resettlement areas. As a consequence, the indigenous inhabitants have begun to witness the change since the temperature of the region has become relatively warmer than before. Moreover, drought occurrences have become more frequent than during the pre-resettlement period. In short, in view of the new grave deforestation process most of the valuable plant species of the region are on the way to being completely depleted.

In order to comprehend more fully the effects of the recent land-use changes on selected valuable plants, an ethno botanical investigation into 23 plant species was conducted.

9.4 Ethno botanical Analysis of the 23 Selected Plants

The selected plant species (Table 12) have been divided into three categories, namely *tree species; tree-crop species; and grass species.* These plant species have been described below from the point of view of their origins, advantages, and cultural attachments to the people; and their status during the pre-and post-resettlement periods. See also Mengistu, 1995a.

Table 12. Selected plant species

SELECTED PLANT SPECIES	LOCAL NAME (ANUAK)	SCIENTIFIC NAMES	FAMILY NAME
Natural Trees	Acheri	Terminalia laxiflora Engl. .& Diels	Combretaceae
	Adekwala	Oncoba spinosa Forssk	Flacourtiaceae
	Adizeqway	Baphia abyssinica Brummitt	Fabaceae
	Aremo	Ziziphus mucronata wild	Rhamnaceae
	Bay Bay	Azadirachta indica L.	Meliaceae
	Chua	Tamarindus indica L.	Fabaceae
	Hadi Dego	Kigelia aethiopicum (Zenz) Dandy	Bignoniaceae
	Kijang	Combretum sp.	Combretaceae
	Kobey	Celtis sp.	Ulmaceae
	Ober	Phyllanthus sp.	Euphorbaceae
	Orogo	Cordia abyssinica R.Br.	Boraginaceae
	Orway	Xylopia parviflora (A Rich.) Benth	Annonaceae
	Pok	Tiliacora aff. funifera (Miers) Oliv.	Menispermaceae
	Tengo	Ficus capreaefolia Del.	Moraceae
	Thoa	Balanites aegyptiaca L.Diels	Balanitaceae
	Thwa	Borassus aethiopum Martius	Palmae
	Udalo	Ficus dicranostyla Mildbr	Moraceae
Crop Trees			
	Mango	Mangifera indica L.	Anacardiaceae
	Papaya	Carica papaya L.	Caricaceae L.
Natural Grass			
	Abaro	Pennisetum purpureum	Poaceae
	Ageda	Panicum sp.	Poaceae
	Akerach	Panicum maximum Jacq.	Poaceae
	Chemcher	Sorghum sp.	Poaceae

9.5 The Tree Species

ACHERI (*Terminalia laxiflora* Engle & Diels).
This is a tall and straight tree, which has a great demand for the construction of such items as houses, granaries, tool-handles, spear-shafts and walking sticks. According to the native people this tree has a chemical defensive system against termites and other animals. The *Acheri* is seldom found in the

Region owing to the spread of resettlements and farm areas. However, it still exists among the traditional farm areas.

ADEKWALA (*Oncoba spinosa Forssk.*).

This is a fast-growing tree growing mostly on flatter areas in central and western Gambela together with scattered shrubs. This tree produces significant quantities of edible fruits. These fruits are useful as supplementary food for the local people. Its dormant seeds remain in the soil for many years if they are not affected either by fire or animals. The fruits are shaded by tree leaves, which grow over them. In the area where deforestation has taken place this deciduous tree does not bear fruits since it requires a specific microclimate condition (e.g. good soil moisture). In the area where grasses and shrubs grow high the canopy of ADEKWALA can be damaged by the occurrence of fires.

ADIZEQWAY (*Baphia abyssinica* Brummitt).

This tree grows in areas that have altitudes ranging from 500-1200 m in Mizan Teferi, Illubabor, Kefa, and Gamo Gofa in Ethiopia and in the Sudan (Hedberg & Edwards (eds), 1989). The thick, straight, tall and broad-leaved trees grow mainly in the central and southern parts of the Gambela plain. The trunk of this tree is soft and sometimes holds rainwater. Its broad dense leaves and easily decayable trunk seem to fertilise the soils. The indigenous people use this tree for making mortars, pestles, and tools and for constructing houses and granaries. Its wood is also used for making toothbrushes.

AREMO (*Ziziphus mucronata* Willd.).

This tree tolerates a wide range of temperature and is found not in the Gambela Region but also in many other parts of the country because the fruits are edible and it is easily spread (Hedberg & Edwards (eds.), 1989). AREMO is evergreen and people and animals enjoy its fruits. It reaches 20 m and provides useful wood for building material. As a fuel-wood species, its yield is estimated at about 25 m^3 per hectare. According to the local people the hard and heavy wood of the AREMO tree is not attractive to termites probably because of its chemical content which acts as a defence. New shoots develop easily from the roots of this tree. Since the wood of AREMO trees have a high demand coupled with the fact that they are affected by the deforestation process they do not grow any more in the areas covered by the resettlement sites and mechanised farms.

BAY BAY, NEEM (*Azadirachta indica* L.).

This tree is introduced from India and is found in some towns below 1,500 m in many parts of the country. The tree can grow up to 4 m in height within a two-year period. It is used for making traditional toothbrushes as well as serving as a windbreak. Its shining and dense foliage attracts visitors and protects houses from wind and dust. The leaves are suspected of containing toxic substances, which prevent flies from entering the houses. The roots and leaves are used as traditional medicine. The fruits contain an important natural insecticide but are not poisonous to people, so the powered seeds can be added to stored grains to reduce attacks by storage insects.

CHUA, TAMARIND (*Tamarindus indica* L.)

This leguminous tree is found not only in the Gambela Region but also in many other areas throughout the country generally below 1,500 m. The tree grows along river courses as its deep roots can access underground water sources. This evergreen tree is impressive and has a large biomass in the well-drained localities, mainly on sandy soils than in other areas. Its evergreen leaves appear to be good for fertilising the soils. Since the CHUA requires many years to reach full growth special care is needed to maintain the old generation and replace them with new ones. It reaches about 25 m in height and the fuel-wood production is estimated to be 120 m³ per hectare. This tree has beautiful flowers, which together with its fruits are used as food and traditional medicine and the wood is useful as timber.

HADI DEGO, SAUSAGE TREE *(Kigelia aethiopicum) (Fenzl) Dandy*

This tree has a height about 25 m and is found between Abobo and Gog-Jor on slopes having a gradient of about 0.1%. It is a deciduous tree, which holds its leaves from February to March and regenerates new leaves during the small rains. It protects itself from fire and herbivores by its height. This tree has dense foliage, which appears to be used for fertilising the soils. The HADI DEGO tree is thick and strong and it is one of the most important trees used for construction purposes.

KIJANG (Combretum sp.)

The oldest and tallest KIJANG tree can reach up to 35 m. The KIJANG trees are found in the old Kir settlement at the foot-hills of the Ukuna Kijang area. The area is named after this tree. This name signifies a land of tall and big trees. The reasons why the oldest and bigest KIJANG trees are found in the Ukuna Kijang area mainly three:

- 'Kir' was one of the headquarters of the traditional nobles and chiefs known as *Nybours* and *Iwaks* respectively. Since the KIJANG tree has been and still is being used as one of the meeting places the tree has been used sustainably.
- The local people make a traditional drink, known as *tej* by mixing honey with the bark of the KIJANG TREE. As *tej* is a drink of the highest rank in the society of the Region and since the KIJANG tree contributes to the making of this drink, the tree is widely known throughout the region; and
- Finally the well-drained soils, the permanent flow of the Chiru River, one of the tributaries of the Alwero River, as well as the absence of browsers and grazers allow the KIJANG tree to increase in number, height and width.

KOBEY (*Celtis* sp.)

This tree is found in both the swampy and non-swampy areas where the land has a 0.5% gradient. The trees reach a height of about 19 m and repetition produce large amounts of wild fruits. The fruits remain on the trees during the dry season when they shed their leaves and branches. This tree loses its leaves a little earlier than other plants. Although the dense ground litter attracts fires, the seeds are protected by the hard cover from being damaged. The seeds normally are induced to germinate by fire or through consumption by wild animals. Otherwise they are likely to remain in the ground without germination for many years.

OBER (*Phyllanthus* sp.)

This tree is mainly located in the less drained areas. It is very sensitive to intensive land-use, which is the main reason why it is not found in the intensively used areas. If there is no other vegetation type growing around this tree it either quickly dies or does not produce leaves. The height of the tree averages less than 10 m and it has unmistakably bright green leaves; the soil around the tree appears fertile. It requires much water for its growth as well as clayey and alluvial soil. It produces large quantities of edible fruits, which are consumed by both humans and animals.

OROGO (*Cordia abyssinica* R. Br.)

This tree grows throughout the country up to 2, 300-m a.s.l. Many OROGO trees are found in the traditional settlement areas in Gambela, but they do not any longer grow in the intensive land-use areas where they used to be grown abundantly. However, large and broad-leaved OROGO trees are grown or found in the Ukuna Kijang area in Eastern Abobo. The heights of the trees growing in the foothills reach 15-20 m and these trees provide greater yields of fruits than those growing at the lower altitudes. The OROGO tree is one of the largest trees in the Gambela landscape. The tree prefers well-drained soils and is vulnerable to fire during its early stages. The traditional people use this tree for making JOYS or canoes, and utensils as well as beehives. This tree also produces large quantities of beautiful and fragrant flowers, from which bees collect nectar and pollen. The tree produces also a considerable amount of sweet edible fruits and it contributes indirectly to the production of high-yield honey. In addition the tree, through its shade, serves as a market place for the local people and as such it has a close linkage with the cultural life of these people.

ORWAY (*Xylopia parviflora* (A.Rich) Benth.)

This tree is located along the waterways of the Gambela Region. It is widespread in Sub-Saharan Africa (Edwards et al., 2000). This evergreen tree is used for making mortars and pestles. This termite-proof tree should to be 10-15 years old before it is used for such purposes as construction of tool-handles. As the demand for this tree is quite high its number has declined considerably in the resettlement sites and farmlands.

POK (*Tiliacora* sp. aff. *funifer* Oliv.)

This plant is found in central Abobo and in areas of Gog and Jor where the gradient is 0.3%. The name POK was derived from the word for 'tall' – KAPOK. The indigenous people use this tree for making *joys*, mortars, pestles and constructing fences. It matures between 15-20 years. Its horizontally growing root biomass occupies a large surface; and birds for constructing their nesting places use the tree branches. Most of the POK trees are, however, found in the clayey and loamy soil area of the central part of the Gambela plain.

TENGO (*Ficus capreaefolia* Del.)

TENGO is a fig tree widespread in tropical African and found throughout the country up to 2600 m (Hedberg & Edwards (eds.), 1989). In the study areas TENGO grows to about 15-m height mainly along rivers and in the central part of the Gambela plain. This tree requires much moisture for its growth. The indigenous people make bark cloth and mallets out of the greyish bark of the trees.

TENGO is one of the most important trees in the Gambela Region. It has a defensive system against fires owing to its height and thick bark. It is also believed to be protected from wild herbivores by its chemical substances. However, when the dry season is extended the thick bark of the tree dries up and it becomes vulnerable to fire outbreaks. This is one of the reasons why the population of this tree is declining, especially during the post-settlement period.

THOA, DESERT DATE (*Balanites aegyptiaca* (L.) Del)

This multi-purpose tree is found in all the drier areas of Ethiopia up to 1,800 m. It is also widespread throughout the Sahel and the Arabian Peninsula (Hedberg & Edwards (eds.), 1989). In the Gambela Region most THOA trees grow in areas below 600 m. It is one of the tallest (19-23 m in height) trees in the region. This tree, which is thorny, semi-deciduous, deep-rooted and thick-barked, produces beautiful flowers, plenty of sweet wild fruits, which are pale brown and are widely consumed by people and wild animals. The seeds are estimated to have an oil-content of 30-40% and some indigenous people use this for making soap and alcoholic beverages. Drugs are also extracted from the bark and fruits and the roots are used as traditional toothbrushes. It is also believed the trees chemical substances can protect it from termites and other predators. It is also highly valued as firewood and produces good quality charcoal. It is reported to live longer than most other trees but it is vulnerable to fire. THOA is one of the species in the Region that has suffered considerably from the change in land-use systems.

THWA *(Borassus aethiopium Martius)*
The THWA is a palm tree with a height of 30-40 m, making it one of the tallest trees in the Gambela plain. Its hard leaves, bark and height protect it from fire and large herbivores. Since it does not have much leafy biomass the tree is suitable for intercropping systems. It produces large fruits with sweet flesh similar to the *Papaya* fruits. The wood and the hard bark are of a high quality suited for the construction of houses, bridges and the like. Prior to the introduction of the resettlement schemes the THWA tree used to be found widely in the Region. However, the resettlement process has negatively affected this valuable tree and hence its total population has gone down significantly.

UDALO *(Ficus dicranostyla Mildbr)*
The maximum height of this tree is around 20 m. Its bark is greyish brown and rough. This tree is well represented in the relatively dense forest areas. The fruits are eaten by wild animals. The local people for making beehives use the trunk, which is wide and often hollow. The tree is also used for making furniture. Those trees that are found in the non-swampy, sandy and loamy soils are much larger than those grown in other localities.

9.6 Tree Crop Species

MAGA, MANGO (Mangifera indica)
The MAGA is a cultivated fruit tree. It is one of the oldest and most important tropical fruit trees. As it is culturally associated with the folklore of the indigenous people it is considered a sacred tree. It is grown on the riverbanks, in resettlement sites, and by water edges. This long-lived tree provides ample fruits to the indigenous people. Along the Baro River two harvesting periods are observed per year. The big or long, thick yellowish-red skinned fruit has a rich flavour and is eaten fresh. The MAGA tree grows up to 10-20 m high and has beautiful evergreen, dark green leaves with impressive small pink flowers. The number of this important tree has been reduced considerably because of the spread of resettlement sites, mechanised farms and urban areas.

PALETAL, PAPAYA (Carica papaya L.)
This is a small cultivated fruit tree. Like other supplementary food crops, such as manioc and pumpkin, the PALETAL fruit is cultivated in the compounds of most of the settlement sites in Gambela. The tree

grows widely and rapidly producing good yields within one or two years. Individual fruits can weigh up to 4 kg, and the people believe that its milky juice gives protection from infection by any type of tropical disease. Like the other trees this is also affected by the development of resettlement schemes and thus its number has decreased greatly.

9.7 The Grass Species

ABARO or KILLO (Penisetum purpureum)
ABARO is one of the elephant grass species grown everywhere in the Gambela Region, mainly at lower altitudes. It grows faster than the AKERACH and AGEDA grasses, which are discussed below. This drought resistant plant grows densely and quickly when it receives adequate rainfall. This plant appears to hold soil particles together and hence it gives the soil good permeability. The indigenous people use ABARO for protecting crops from being eaten by birds. The local people also use ABARO for fencing their houses. Its abundant litter appears to increase the soils' organic matter. If it is well managed it can be used as fodder as well as for making furniture and for fringing terraces in order to reduce runoff.

AKERACH (Panicum maximum Jacq.)
AKERACH is one of the most important grasses used for house construction. This high quality and tall (1-3 m) grass has the capacity to protect people from the belligerent tropical rainfalls. It grows in all types of soils with or without scattered trees. As elsewhere, the introduction of the resettlement schemes has brought a reduction of the quantity of this type of grass. Moreover, its shallow roots have exposed it to fires, grazing, trampling and tractor-farming.

AGEDA (Panicum sp.)
This is similar to AKERACH and it grows in all parts of the Region. Like the other types of grasses this grass re-sprouts in April and remains green between May and September, but it dries up between October and March, which makes it vulnerable to fire. The straw is useful for thatching houses and granaries, and for making sweeping brushes. Like the other types of grasses the AGEDA is a good source of fodder. Although it has a deep rooting system it is not protected from being damaged by the intensive land-use systems in the Region.

CHEMCHER (Sorghum sp.)
CHEMCHER is a grass species that is smaller and less stiff than ABARO. It changes its colour between October and November and becomes sensitive to fire when it dries up. It grows throughout the Region and has broad and dense leaves. This grass is used for thatching houses and granaries as well as for making mats and constructing fences. CHEMCHER requires little rain for its growth and hence it is drought-resistant.

The above-mentioned plant species have been well managed in the traditional settlements but the resettlement schemes and mechanised farms have negatively affected them.

9.8 SUMMARY

Through sustainable land-use methods, using rudimentary farming tools and long-fallow periods, the indigenous people have produced fruits, leaves and root biomass, probably for hundreds of years. In contrast the resettlement schemes have caused deforestation which has reduced the populations of these selected plants in the last 20 years. Compare Figures 23 and 24.

Figure 23. Traditional settlement, food and non-food biomass before the resettlement schemes.

Figure 24. Cotton crop in the mechanised farmland after the resettlement schemes

(The author is in the middle of the cotton farmland in 1991)

Research shows that the organic matter, total nitrogen, available potassium and phosphorus have declined in the mechanised farms, but have remained at a high level in the traditional settlement sites. The destruction of the plant cover "may lead to both chemical and physical changes in the soil as well as increased erosion"(Hösier, 1988:123). However, the losses could be redeemed depending upon the clearing and burning methods chosen and post-fire land management practices. In an ecosystem-stability study in a humid tropical climate, Hill (1987) contended that a forest cleared and burnt by traditional methods and by bulldozers, will take about 22 years and 100 years, respectively, to re-accumulate biomass.

Misdirected decisions and planning endeavours, absence of workable environmental protective measures and political unrest in the country appear to be the fundamental causes of deforestation. These problems have not been addressed seriously by the previous and present governments of the country. However, one obvious fundamental hurdle ought to be pointed out in this respect. As long as widespread and deep-rooted poverty prevails throughout the country it is nearly impossible to implement an environmental protection law even if it is potentially flawless.

The previous government had formulated two contradictory policies. On the one hand there were nation-wide water, soil and forest conservation programmes. On the other hand there was another policy which advocated the destruction of the original vegetation in order to make room for the resettlers (Mengistu, 1986).

As Robert Lamb (quoted by Wljkman, 1984:38) noted on the seriousness of the environmental crisis in Ethiopia, the highland regions "have been so over-farmed, overgrazed and deforested that efforts to scrape a bare living from this land threaten to destroy it permanently". The same process of deforestation is being observed in the Gambela region. Like the people in the highland region the resettlers here also depended heavily on the local resources. They cut and burn the plants and farm the land intensively without crop rotation. Moreover, various fruits are collected from the trees and wood is cut for the purposes of energy and the construction of houses, beds, fences, and utensils. Since the wood and agricultural land have become scarce the resettlers have to travel long distances to obtain them. Consequently the indigenous people and the resettlers are loosing very fast their resources which are the bases of their sustenance.

10 CHAPTER 10: THE EFFECTS OF FIRES ON THE PLANT COMMUNITIES AND SOILS

Fires are described as natural (wild), uncontrolled, controlled (human-induced), forest, bush, grass, ground and crown fires. The intensity and frequency of fires depend on the topographical features, temperature, rainfall, and wind direction and vegetation types, among others, of an area or region. Humans and certain types of animals have the possibility to escape from fire, but plants remain exposed to fire occurrences. All vegetation types are not devastated equally by fire in all parts of the world (Duncan & Brown, 1995). They differ from being fire-sensitive to fire-tolerant and fire-resistant, or able to recover from the destructive effects. Plants can be damaged wholly or partially, permanently or temporarily depending on the following factors (Dansereau (1957): (a) time and space; (b) frequency and intensity of fires; (c) weather conditions at the time of burning and post-burning; (d) ground cover; (e) soil types; and (f) land-use patterns.

Fire serves as an important ecosystem management technique that is widely used by many people in tropical regions. Fire is the most potent environmental factor which shapes the natural vegetation in the African continent (cited by Oba, 1990). In Ethiopia, fires have been used to clear land to grow crops and to improve the grazing grounds for livestock. Poor farmers use bush or forest fires in order to clear farmland for growing food crops. These farmers include those peasants who: (a) depend mainly on the livestock; (b) use hoe-farming due to farming tradition and lack of oxen; and (c) do not have sufficient farmland or have difficulties either to buy oxen or fertilisers, or get manure and transport it to their fields or farms. Fires are used for similar purposes in Gambela.

10.1 The Effects of Fires on the Plant Communities and Soils in the Gambela Region

The Gambela Region is generally fire-prone, sparsely populated, relatively underdeveloped and environmentally sensitive. The causes and effects of fires in the region vary from one place to another. In general, however, the present morphology and physiognomy of the plant species in the region have probably resulted from repeated fires (see Mengistu, 1998 and Minassie, 2000). The previous forestlands, as a result, have been converted into woody, grassy and bushy lands. Moreover, the following grave consequences have resulted: a significant reduction of certain plant species and the forced migration of wild animals to neighbouring country.

Two types of fires can be identified in the Gambela Region, namely the naturally caused uncontrolled fires and the human-induced controlled fires.

10.1.1 The naturally-caused uncontrolled fires

These are caused by lightning at the beginning of the rainy season. During the dry season, the region is covered with dense and tall dry grasses. At the same time the trees loose their leaves, which accumulate on the ground. The local people use some of these as fuel. The uncontrolled fires are common in the natural forests, grasses and bushes.

The intensity of fires normally becomes high when the weather is hot and dry during the months of December and May, and dies down after May when the temperature declines. Since there are no strong winds during the dry-season and since the fires are often uncontrolled it is hard to tell their direction and spread. Winds serve the following purposes, to: (a) predict the direction of the fires; (b) shorten the fire period; (c) increase heat; and (d) spread the seeds to distant places.

Strong winds occur when the ground is covered with vegetation i.e. between August and September. When a fire starts somewhere one first observes the rising clouds -followed by flames which can stay longer if old and dead trees sustain them. Some trees have thick bark and chemical substances that can protect them from fires and wild herbivores. In some plants, such as *Ficus capreaefolia*, flames cause holes in the trees, which are used by bees as beehives and birds for nesting. In the process, however, the indigenous people are deprived of their valuable benefits such as medicaments, bark-clothes, mallets, dyes, timber and firewood. Moreover, when a burning tree falls down the flames go deep into the soil profile and burn the organic matter of the soil. In essence, this kills the fertility of the soils. Examine the appearance of the vegetation during the pre- and post- fire periods in Figures 25 and 26. The dry matter is burnt first and is replaced by different types of vegetation. Although it is not known for certain to what extent fires destroy the natural vegetation and drive out the wild life, it is believed generally that the Gambela Region still retains a considerable biodiversity (Mengistu, 1995a). As soon as the fire outbreaks are over grasses, especially *Pennisetum purpureum* and *Panicum maximum*, begin to sprout even without rain owing to the residual soil moisture. With a little rainfall numerous seeds germinate and quickly re-vegetate the fire-affected areas. The accumulated dead biomass or fuel remains buried until the next fire occurs since it is unpalatable.

Figure 25. Effects of uncontrolled forest-grass fire during the dry season (1994).

Figure 26. Post-fire vegetation during the dry season (1994)

As Whelan (1995) argued, revegetation requires time, and depends of the availability of seed banks in the ground or soils, soil moisture and nutrients, among other factors. Phillips (1975) observed that in the sub-humid savannah tropics early burning, especially during the dry-season, causes severe damage to seed banks as well as to newly grown and big trees. Although some of the wild fruits in the Gambela Region, such as *Balanites aegyptiaca*, mature during the post-fire period, most of the plants such as *Celtis* sp. and wild *Ziziphus* mature early. Early fire incidences, therefore, affect these beautiful flower buds and plenty of sweet wild fruits. As Parsons (1976) argued fire is one of the determining factors for the development of certain types of seed germination, especially for the plants that have already adapted to fire. There are also other types of seed, which respond to fire by sprouting. As observed in the field most of the fruits and seeds have hard shells and can only be spread either through fire or animals. Without the occurrence of fire, plant populations might be low, and fresh and good grass biomass would have not been available for the herbivores.

The morphology of plants and geometry of leaves are affected by the precipitation and fire. In the high grass dominated areas in the western parts most of the trees are not straight but in the eastern parts of the region the trees are straighter. In the western parts, the fires have high intensity while this is lower in the tree-dominated broad leaf zones in the eastern part of the region.

10.1.2 The human-induced controlled fires

The indigenous people use fire for the following purposes to: (a) improve hunting; (b) enable footpaths and directions to be easily identified; (c) reduce population of weeds; (d) grow crops; (e) enhance vigorous grass growth in the rainy seasons; (f) drive away animals that are dangerous to crop plants; (g) protect settlements from high fire; (h) remove dead plants, crop residues and pests; (i) evict bees before raiding their hives for honey; and (j) make charcoal. However, controlled fires often turn into uncontrolled ones. In some areas, fires are lit after sundown when there is less wind. In some areas the indigenous people burn grasses when there is still moisture in the vegetation rather than during the dry season as this reduces the intensity of the burn, which causes the greatest risk of widespread fire. Another fire management practice is also applied to the plots where crops have been harvested. The farmers gather old stalks into piles and burn them at the end of the dry-season. When the soil is exhausted at a farm site the farmers move to other farm-sites in order to allow the original farm-site to regenerate its nutrients.

Burning in the mechanised farms has been performed irregularly and intensively depending on the instructions provided by the local authorities. In order to resettle people the bulldozers may be used to pull down trees which are then burnt. To prepare the land for the next harvest the resettlers and agricultural workers cut down regenerating bushes, grasses and trees and burn them any time during the dry-period. See Figure 27.

Figure 27 Cutting grasses and bushes before burning (1998).

Note: Not many big trees were found after two years of deforestation. Trees were replaced by bush and grass species, and it requires intensive labour to prepare the land for the coming crop season.

Based on the soil samples taken at the end of a fire period in the Gambela Region it was found that grasslands contained lower soil nutrients than forestlands owing to the negative impact of fires on the soils. Daubennire (1968) argued that regular burning in the grassland ecosystem increases soil nutrients in the form of ashes.

As pointed out by Moore (1996), fire has both rejuvenating properties as well as damaging effects on soil properties and plant species. These effects can: (a) affect the development of vegetation and ecosystem succession; (b) releases of nutrients from the litter and biomass; (c) stimulate seeds to germinate and seedlings to establish; and (d) interrupt the restoration of useful microbial function in the soils. On the other hand, fire causes the loss of oxygen from the soil, reduces cation exchange capacity and increases soil temperature.

As reported by Young (1976) in his study of tropical soils, clearing the natural vegetation, burning and using the land for intensive cultivation purposes causes a decline in the soil organic matter and nutrients stored in it. This process coincides with the losses of nitrogen, sulphur and carbon to the atmosphere and leads to internal and surface leaching during the first rains. This may be one of the reasons why soil organic matters, phosphorous; potassium and nitrogen in the mechanised farmlands are lower in comparison to the traditional farmlands and forestlands.

Some fire-related erosion signs have already been observed on the mechanised farms and settlement sites. The natural vegetation is indiscriminately cleared and burnt. Ross et al. (1990), from their study in northern Brazil, argued that the removal of forest cover leads to instability in the soil cover and this in turn leads to soil erosion and loss of productivity in the entire environment affected by this process. Fires not only destroy the natural trees and tree crops but also devastate the natural habitat of wildlife that could have been important sources of income for the local people, in particular, and the national economy, in general.

On the whole, burning by itself is not destructive but essential in the formation of major types of vegetation in special ecological zones. If, for example, the removal of accumulated humus and litter becomes necessary the use of fire is vital and the ashes in turn are valuable for fertilising the soils. Fire is also important or necessary to control weeds, insects and fungi, modify the physico-chemical environment of the plants, and stimulate seed germination, rapid growth, flowering and fruiting (Stamp, 1964 and Stromgaard, 1988.). Nevertheless, lack of proper fire management technique, such as applying fire belt methods before burning as well as the implementation of post-fire and post-harvest land management systems, can lead to the depletion of soil nutrients.

10.2 SUMMARY

When fire devastates a virgin land, it disturbs all the animal and plant species. Although fire reduces the numbers of many plant species, sometimes even leading to extinction, there is also the creation of a fire-adapted ecosystem. Fire occurrences gradually change the structure, physiognomy, regeneration, and composition of animal and plant species, hydrological cycle, soil structure and nutrients. The fire-induced environment is distinct and is sharpened every year by fire occurrences. Such distinction can be observed on the boundary between the savannah and high forests or rainforests in many parts of Africa. The already fire-adapted indigenous plant and animal species require fire for their survival, reproduction and regeneration.

As observed in the Gambela Region during high-intensity fire periods, all the plants and animals seem to be consumed by fire, but most trees protect themselves by their heights, hard bark and deep rooting systems. For instance, *Borassus aethiopum* protects itself from fires and herbivores by its hard leaves, hard bark and height. Even though the *Pennisetum purpureum* grass is sensitive to fire it survives through its deep rooting systems. Some animals like elephants, lions and buffaloes migrate, and others take refugee, and still others like rats and snakes hide in the physically cracking vertisols. When fire changes the existing ecosystem, animal and plant species also search for new survival strategies. As soon as the fire is stopped by rain, the ground surface is quickly covered with dense grasses, regenerating trees, newly growing trees, bushes and herbs. In short, fire is part of the ecological balancing mechanism. Generally animal and plant species as well as micro organisms of the Gambela Region seem to have adapted to live in harmony with fire regimes.

The crucial question that ought to be raised is how long can the Gambela ecosystem tolerate the uncontrolled fire regimes and the resulting mismanagement of the natural resources? Unless the effects of burning on the natural resources of the region are counteracted by appropriate post-fire management techniques the conflict between the natural and human ecosystems is likely to be aggravated.

11 CHAPTER 11: THE EFFECTS OF FIRE AND WAR RELATED INCIDENCES ON THE WILDLIFE IN THE BARO-AKOBO (GAMBELA) AND PIBOR-SOBAT SUDAN RIVER BASINS

As a result of the refugee settlement and resettlement schemes, and other land-use changes, the wildlife and their natural habitats have been gravely affected along the Baro-Akobo and Pibor-Sobat river basins. The term wildlife refers to life forms that are neither domesticated nor cultivated. Biodiversity is the sum of life forms at all levels of organisation in biological systems. Biodiversity loss includes, among other things, the over-exploitation of wildlife. Wildlife utilisation requires sustainable uses of organisms, which can be achieved through the effective protection of natural habitats, including soils and water (Myers, 1995, Rodgers, 1992). There is a significant move towards conservation of endangered wildlife species (Noss, 1991).

Wildlife conservation can be achieved through community-based sustainable utilisation of natural resources or habitats. If habitats are conserved, wildlife can be used as a viable land-use option which can: (a) contribute to the recovery, maintenance and improvement of all ecosystems; (b) provide food, medicines, ornaments, and cash, in the form of tourism; (c) create jobs in the wildlife sector; and (d) enhance regional development.

Although ecologists, national and international agencies such as the IUCN (the International Union for the Conservation of Nature), WWF (World Wide Fund for Nature) and Green Peace, advocate the safeguarding of wild animals, wildlife is still being destroyed legally and illegally (Duncan, 1992). According to Gore (1989), the extinction of natural habitats is acute. Man has always been an effective as well as an 'intelligent' predator. The destruction of biodiversity or habitat will cause the extinction of wildlife affecting humans as well.

The degree of local extinction appears to be fast, due to (a) the destruction of natural habitats caused by human population explosion, settlement and land-use changes; (b) political, ethnic and resource-use conflicts; and (c) the easy access to automatic weapon and flow of illegal trade. The latter is due to demands from developed countries. The nomads, pastoralists, farmers and even people from urban areas in developing countries supply wildlife products. Moreover, important issues such as what, how, where and when to conserve wildlife have not been studied. In savannah ecology, for example, the conservation of wildebeest species should be given first priority. Since this species maintains grassland in a sustainable manner, it is useful for the survival of other grass-eating animals. These, in turn, provide sources of food for predatory animals. Human-induced climatic change aggravates widespread fires and floods. These have negative effects on national parks, reserves and sanctuaries that are refugee for many wildlife species.

Wildlife is both structurally and functionally an integral part of the whole ecosystem. It is a natural resource for national and international communities. As a result, there is an urgent need for regional and global co-operation to safeguard and protect the wildlife and their habitats as well as conserve other elements of biodiversity.

11.1 The Absolute and Relative Locations of the Study Area

The area studied stretches between the lower Baro-Akobo River basin in Gambela, south-western Ethiopia and the Pibor-Sobat River basin in southern Sudan (Figure 28), i.e. approximately between 7° 00'N and 8° 37' N latitude and 32° 00'E and 35° 00'E longitude. Since wildlife does not recognise politico-geographic borders, they move back and forth between the two river basins. The two basins include all rivers draining from the Ethiopian highlands to the Pibor-Sobat River basin, the Sobat being a tributary of the White Nile; the humid-tropical savannah slopes ranging from 300 to 1000 m a.s.l.; and the flood plain ecosystem with mainly heavy clay soils (vertisols and ferralsols). The mean annual average temperature of the area varies from 25°C to 39°C, rainfall (high rainfall occurs from May to October) from 750 to 2000 mm, and relative humidity from 60% to 87%.

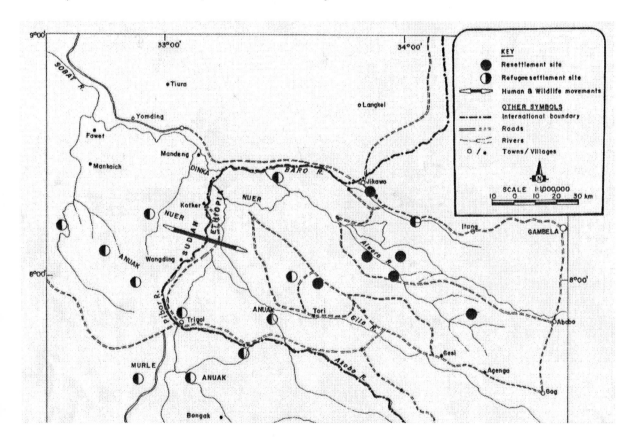

Figure 28. Absolute and relative locations of the study area

The vegetation comprises xerophyllous open woodlands, forests, tree savannah and grasses.
The indigenous peoples are the Anuak and Nuer of Nilotic origin who are sparsely settled in the area. The Murle and Dinka inhabit the Pibor-Sobat river basin. The Anuaks comprise the majority and are engaged in simple farming using hoes. They are also hunters and gatherers. The Nuer and Murle are engaged in livestock husbandry, as well as hunting and some farming activities. Although human and

125

wildlife population movements between the two river basins are an ecological phenomenon, forced migration processes are due to political and socio-economic conditions.

11.2 The Spatial Distribution of Wildlife

An unusual abundance of mammals was observed along the Baro-Akobo and Pibor-Sobat river basin. A list of wild animal species along the Ethiopian-Sudanese border is given in Table 13.

Table 13. List of wild animal species along the Ethiopian-Sudanese border

Family	English Name	Scientific Name
Hipposiderinae	Sundevals African Leaf-nosed Bat	*Hipposideros caffer*
Erinaceidae	White-bellied Hedgehog	*Atelerix albiventris*
Seluri Squirrels	Geoffrey's Ground Squirrel	*Kerus erythropus*
Thryonomidae	Lesser Cane Rat	*Thryonomys gregorianus*
Hystricidae	Crested Pocupihe	*Hystrix cristata*
Cercopithecidae	Patas monkey	*Erythrocebus patas*
-	Blue monkey	*Cercopithecus mitis*
-	Grivet monkey	*C. aethiops cynocephlus*
-	Anubis Baboon	*Papio anubis*
Colobidae	Guereza	*Colobus guereza*
Mustelidae	Ratel	*Mellivora capensis*
Canidae	African Hunting Dog	*Lycaon pictus*
Viverridae	African Civet	*Cvettictics civetta*
-	Common Genet	*Genetta tigrina*
-	Marsh Mongoose	*Atilax paludinosus*
-	Southern Dwarf Mongoose	*Helogale hirhula*
-	Slender Mongoose	*Galerella sanguinea*
Protelidae	Aardwolf	*Proteles cristatus*
Hyaenidae	Spotted Hyaena	*Crocuta crocuta*
Felidae	Wildcat	*Felis sylvestris*
-	Serval	*Leptailurus serval*
-	Caracal	*Caracal Caracal*
-	Leopard	*Panthera pardus*
-	Lion	*P. leo*
Hippopotamidae	Hippopotamus	*Hippopotamus amphibius*
Suidae	Giant Forest Hog	*Hylochoerus meinertzhageni*
-	Bush Pig	*Potamochoerus larvatus*
-	Warthog common	*Phacochoerus africanus*
Giraffidae	Giraffe	*Giraffa camelopardalis*

Family	English Name	Scientific Name
Bovidae	Jaksson Hartebeest	Alcelaphus buselaphus
-	Tiang	Damaliscus lunatus
-	Bush Duiker	Sylvicapra grimmia
-	Oribi	Ourebia ourebi
-	White-Eared Kob	Kobus kop leucotis
-	Nile Lechwe	Kobus megaceros
-	Waterbuck	Kobus ellipsiprymnus
-	Bohor Reedbuck	Redunca redunca
-	Roan antelope	Hippotragus equinus
-	Bushbuck	Tragelaphus scriptus
-	Buffalo	Syncerus caffer
Elephantidae	African Elephant	Loxodonta africana
Procaviidae	Rock Hyrax	Procavia capensis

Note: Nile Lechwe and White-Eared Kob are found only in the two river basins.
Source: Hillman, 1993.

Palaearctic migratory bird species, especially waders, Egyptian Goose, Sacred Ibis, Egrets, Kingfishers, Pelican, aquatic and swamp bird species were also noticed during the survey. Interaction and dependence between the indigenous people and wildlife, the effects of war on wildlife species and their habitats were also observed.

The spatial distribution, concentration and movement of wild animals over the two river basins is associated with (a) alternating rainy and dry seasons; (b) flat (muddy and sticky) and mountain topographical and hydro-physical features; (c) availability and scarcity of water and nutrient-poor or nutrient-rich vegetation species; (d) settlement and land-use patterns; and (e) the degree of agricultural development, hunting, bush-forest fires and conflicts. Nile lechwe, African elephant and African wild dog, for example, occupy a variety of habitats, including savannah, forests, swampy and the various rivers in the two basins. Their local and regional migration varies from the resting-places to the feeding and watering places depending on the season, bush and grass fires, and the extent of flooding, availability of food resources, and the handling of environmental stress by each individual animal. Predators such as wildcat, lion and leopard are common and spend most of their time on the non-wet areas, savannah and deciduous forests, respectively. They all seem to have a remarkable environmental adaptation strategy. Other carnivores, such as Aardwolf and wild dog, are dispersed throughout the scattered tree areas.

Water and reed buck are mostly found near the rivers, while buffalo, roan antelope, tiang, and bush buck, are found mainly on open grassland and avoid swamps and forests. Giraffe and ostrich *(Struthio caelus)* and tufted guinea-fowl *(Numida meleagris)*, are scattered in woodland savannah areas and migrate from one river basin to another. Some herbivores prefer the flat topography of the grassland and watering sites. Hippopotamus and crocodile live part of the time in water and part of the time on river shores, in lakes and on swampy land surfaces. High densities of poisonous and non-poisonous snake species, rodents (e.g. mice), tortoises and active termites (termite hills up to 3 m with the diameter of base of 6 to 8 m) were found in most places, especially during the wet season. Snakes create difficulties for human movement and activities at the end of the rainy season. Wild animals, such as anubis baboons, vervet monkeys and bush pigs that depend on wild fruits, and roots, and domestic animals spend most of their time at relatively higher altitudes, in savannah woodlands and in less fire-prone areas, as well as around settlement sites.

11.3 Wildlife Ecological Cycle

One of the most interesting features that occur within the study region is the regular seasonal movement of certain species. The wildlife paths go in meridional direction, connecting watering points and seasonally flooded savannah where they can find fresh food, etc. Thousands of White-Eared Kob and many African elephants, for example, migrate from the extreme southwest, south and south-eastern Sudan to Gambela plain during the dry season, returning to the Sudan again at the beginning of the rainy season.

Information provided by local people and the author's observations indicate that the pre-1980s spatial distribution, and migration patterns of wild animals has been completely disrupted. It is now no longer dependent on the ecological cycle, but is determined by the post-1980s developments, particularly the construction of the Abobo dam, the large-scale resettlements, and mechanised farms. These phenomena have led to a serious decline in the numbers and diversity of the wildlife. Particularly destructive have been (a) ideology-related widespread wars, poverty, hunger and resource-use conflicts; (b) unsustainable land-use activities in refugee settlements and resettlement schemes; (c) mis-management of natural habitats, deforestation and extent of fires; and (d) lack of biodiversity conservation measures. As a result, the indigenous peoples suffer from loss of wildlife products, fishing grounds, fruits and root food.

11.4 Habitat destruction

The author observed numerous wild animals roaming around and enjoying forest and grassland in the middle of the 1980s in many parts of the Region, but in 1997 these natural areas were fragmented and some of the animals (e.g. African elephants and White-Eared Kob) were rarely to be seen in the region. The 2001 survey by Minassie et al. (2001) shows that White-Eared Kob was found only in Gog and Jor districts (Table 14).

Table 14. Wildlife counted in some parts of the study region, 2001

District	WEK	Oibi	PM	CB	WH	CM	WTM	LK	WB	VM	GS	AB	BD	SC
Jor	97	-	49	-	-	-	-	-	.	-.	-	-	-	-
Gog	18	-	1	-	-	7	-	-	-	1	42	-	2	-
Abobo	-	-	34	2	2	14	2	-	-	1	62	2	-	2
Itang	-	2	-	-	-	-	-	2	4	-	50	-	1	-
Gambela	-	-	-	1	-	2	-	-	-	-	15	-	1	-
Total	115	2	84	3	2	23	2	2	4	2	169	2	4	2

WEK stands for White earned kob, Oribi, PM - Patas monkey, CB - Common Bushbuck, WH - Warthog, **CM** - Black and white colobus Monkey, WTM -White tailed mongoose, LK - Lesser kudu,

WB - Waterbuck, **VM** - Vervet monkey, GS - Ground squirrel, AB - Anubis baboon, BD - Bush duiker, SC - Serval cat.
Source: Minassie et al. 2001.

As shown in the same table, none of the large animals, such as elephants, were found in the surveyed areas. It seems that wildlife habitat is being destroyed at an alarming rate, indicating that even the present common wildlife species may be endangered after a decade. All that can be said is that a steadily declining number of the above mentioned animals seen in the study region are consistent with circumstantial information suggesting a high hunting pressure associated with conflicts and unsustainable land-use activities. Thus in all aspects of conservation, the responsible bodies in the study region must develop a much greater sense of urgency and determination to save this disappearing heritage.

In the past, the indigenous peoples were well adapted to sustain the biophysical environment, which they utilised through shifting cultivation with simple agricultural techniques, hunting with spears, simple fishing and gathering-collecting activities. Through traditional knowledge and a sustainable land-use system, the indigenous peoples conserved the plant and wildlife ecosystems, soils and bio-physical-cultural landscapes of the Region. The traditional land-use system had 3 purposes: (a) to produce crops for the households; (b) to reduce prevalence of and access to tsetse flies, malaria-transmitting mosquitoes and fire-protection belts by opening the fields (plots) around the settlements; (c) to be able to hunt wild animals in the woodlands around the plots.

Small holders in the Region use small plots to produce maize, and sorghum etc., and the plants and wildlife in the forest provides them with meat, medicine, skins, hides, horns and tail hairs (which are used to make necklaces), furs and feathers. Animals also return phosphorus (P) and nitrogen (N) through their dung and urine to the natural ecosystem. It was observed in the field that through their extensive grazing and browsing behaviour, they seem to regulate the plant composition and they also seem to be one of the main agents for seed distribution, germination and regeneration of tree species.

Due to the intensification of war and land-use changes since the 1980s, the forests and grasses (the staple forage) in certain areas were felled or burned and replaced by refugee settlements and large-scale farms. The total exploitation of the environment has been the greatest general threat to the diversity of wildlife species, an obstacle to safeguarding their habitats and biodiversity, and to the practice of nature conservation. For example, safeguarding wildlife, managing the natural resources and conserving indigenous culture was not the objective of the 1984 resettlement programme on the Ethiopian side, but was rather to resettle people from the drought, wars and famine-affected areas of the highlands in the north to the lowland areas of the country. From the total of more than 600,000 people who resettled in the lowland areas of the country, more than 25% were resettled in the Baro-Akobo river basin. The programme was based on the assumption that the abundance of arable land and water resources in the region would provide self-sufficiency and surplus production without a detailed investigation of the natural resources being undertaken beforehand.

As a consequence of the war and continued conflict in southern Sudan, 300,000 refugees from the same region were also resettled on the Ethiopian side in 1988. More refugee camps and relief sites were also established along the Pibor-Sobat river basin and in the forested areas of Itang, Pugnydo (north of the Gilo River), etc. and in the lower Baro-Akobo river basin (Figure 28). As a result, vast tracts of useful indigenous trees and riparian woodlands were cleared for farming land, refugee settlements, and the establishment of resettlement sites, firewood, and charcoal and construction timber. The results were unpredictable and have had long-lasting impacts on the region's wildlife resource. In areas where wildlife drink water, a dam, for example, was constructed on one of the major wildlife corridors at the Alwero river on the Ethiopian side, and from this reservoir, a long irrigation channel was made, into which many wildlife fell and eventually drowned.

Frequent forest and grass burning to clear land for cropping and for hunting purposes caused habitat destruction in the region, and resulted in loss of forage, and animal habitats, especially for the young animals, and reptiles that could not run away from the fires, and, to some extent, also to soil organisms and soil nutrients (Mengistu, 1996). The present vegetation species are well adapted to fire. Consequently, wildlife has followed the fire cycle for many generations and has adapted to the region's ecosystem. It was observed that when fire occurs, wildlife move to the non-fire areas such as along rivers and into the montane forest, and as soon as the fire stops they return to get new and fresh shoots, and the predators also returned. However, the frequency, intensity and magnitude of the present fire environment of the region are not conducive to wildlife and their habitats. In short, the dramatic decline in the numbers of wildlife and their habitats, therefore, is closely connected with the ongoing war/conflicts, intensity of bush-forest and grass fires, land-use and settlement changes (associated with population increase), poorly planned resettlement schemes and rapid growth of urban centres. These situations have forced wildlife to abandon the natural and seasonal migration cycle and expose themselves to intensive hunting and poaching.

11.5 Poaching Activities

With intimate knowledge of the locations, traditional laws and regulations, hunting was earlier mainly for subsistence and exclusively with spears. It was a very important part of the indigenous peoples' way of life. However, the sustainable hunting culture was disturbed by poaching associated with the: (a) colonial administration; (b) on-going wars and conflicts; (c) loss of traditional institutions and unsustainable government regulation; (d) the introduction of modern weapons; (e) displacement and refugee settlements, and (f) the establishment of resettlements.

According to information gathered from local people and officials, the destruction of wildlife refuges resulted in the failure of wildlife to survive, since they were exposed to their natural enemy - humans. In the 1950s, for example, the British colonial rule in southern Sudan provided weapons to the Oromo highlanders on the Ethiopian side in order to profit from the sales of ivory and skins, which disturbed the sustainable relationships between the indigenous people, wildlife and the natural habitats. Territorial conflicts between and among the indigenous peoples of Anuak-Nuer, Nuer-Dinka and Anuak-Murle were aggravated by the political contradictions among the Anyanya-rebels, SPLM (Sudan People's Liberation Movement), SPLA (Sudan People's Liberation Army), GPLM (Gambela People's Liberation Movement) and GPLF (Gambela People's Liberation Front). As observed in the field, the previous government of Ethiopia allowed the SPLA (the dominant political force in the region) to use the Baro-Akobo basin (Gambela) as a training centre, army base and refugee settlement sites which attracted the flow of automatic weapons into the whole region.

Wildlife was attacked on different fronts. In Southern Sudan, illegal and legal wildlife utilisation and civil war seriously threatened wildlife resources, interrupting the seasonal migration cycle. When government hunting regulations restrained indigenous hunting methods, the number of elephants increased in the limited areas on the Ethiopian side in the 1960s, and damaged crops. Because of this, local farmers appealed to the Wildlife Organisation. In order to reduce the number of elephants, this organisation scared away and indiscriminately killed elephants (Figure 29). Except for ivory, neither the meat nor the skins of the elephants were properly used.

Figure 29 An elephant killed by a wildlife officer

Source: Photo Lealem, 1967

In order to acquire foreign currency, the socialist government (1974-1991) in Ethiopia allowed, under specific licences, foreign visitors to kill elephants for their ivory. When the same government introduced a large-scale resettlement scheme and obliterated wildlife habitats in the 1980s, wildlife were forced to migrate during the wrong seasons and to non-conducive ecological zones. When the indigenous institutions were weakened by the on-going war, intended government policies, and due to lack of sustainable wildlife management techniques and environmental protection measures, refugee settlements and resettlement schemes became established all over the region, which has led to severe deforestation and poaching practises in the two river basins.

When the soldiers, refugees and indigenous people who remained in some areas of the region, together with those in the refugee settlements and resettlement sites faced starvation, the sustainable utilisation of wildlife and sustainable laws of coexistence between the natural resources and humans could no longer be respected, leading to the killing of large numbers of wildlife, both for food and for commercial purposes. The previous conflicts were mainly between the simple hunters (pastoralists and small farmers), but the present conflicts are to acquire as much meat as possible, for example from the White-Eared Kob, other antelopes and elephants. Although attempts have been made to alleviate problems of human refugees, famine and war, hardly any organisations have tried to protect the endangered wildlife species or have undertaken projects directed at conservation of natural resources.

Wildlife in the region should be seen as environmentally sound and economically viable natural resources. Presently, indigenous biodiversity conservation methods are not maintained nor have other alternative strategies been introduced. Instead, everybody is now mining wildlife and their habitats due to the absence of strong indigenous institutions to defend wildlife rights and long-term planning of biodiversity protection measures. These situations have forced not only the wildlife but also the indigenous peoples to be environmental refugees within their own geographical territories.

11.6 The Need for Biodiversity and Habitat Conservation Strategies

The Baro-Akobo and Pibor-Sobat river basins, which have always had the reputation of hosting great numbers of wildlife, were one of the richest wildlife regions in Africa and the best hunting areas in the world (Blower, 1977; Lealem, 1991; Duncan, 1992; EMO, 1978; ENA, 1988 and EVDSA, 1988). In these natural landscapes, the number of wildlife on the Ethiopian side varied from the highest density of more than 50 wild animals per 1000 hectares to the lowest density of 2 per 1000 hectares in the region (EVDSA, 1990 and Hillman, 1993). As observed in the field and discussed with local peoples and officials in the Region, it is the indigenous utilisation of wildlife and their habitats, such as forests and grasses (the source of wild roots and fruits, medicaments, forage and favourable shelters, etc.) that is most badly affected by the present state of affairs. This is due to the concentration of massive refugee settlements and resettlement sites in environmentally vulnerable sites and the associated war and conflicts among peoples, as well as between nature and the users.

How can wildlife be protected and conserved in a Region where there is on-going war and where there are neither compromises nor short or long-term planning strategies for conservation? Like human refugees, wildlife have to be protected and their habitats must be respected through emergency management plans, negotiations and active participation by local peoples, as well as regional, national and international organisations. With the active support and involvement of the WWF and IUCN, it should be possible to convince regional and national governments, international and national organisations, and financial institutions to provide viable funds to cover protection and management costs.

Since wildlife, for many generations, has been the indispensable resource of indigenous peoples in the Region, wild animals and their habitats have been protected through indigenous institutional mechanisms, spiritual-care, sustainable management, and selective and seasonal hunting methods.

Through natural resources management systems, they maintained the local biodiversity and recognised long ago that it would be a great disaster if humans destroyed the environment to which every plant and animal species belongs. They also understood that wildlife utilisation was a viable land-use option since large-scale farming and livestock rising were not conducive to the region's long-term ecosystem, particularly since wildlife survived and multiplied in the region more successfully than domestic livestock. As was estimated by Blower (1977) and EVDSA (1988), wildlife such as buffaloes and antelopes are resistant to the sleeping sickness carried by tsetse flies, and consequently their meat yield per one hectare of pasture is higher as compared with cattle. However, such early warnings were not, and still are not, heeded.

In order to establish quick and concrete wildlife rescue agreements and measures, an understanding between the SPLA, Gambela administrators and the indigenous peoples in particular, as well as the Ethiopian and Sudan governments in general, are urgently needed. If short and long-term wildlife-habitat protection and biodiversity conservation strategies are to be introduced and implemented, permanent peace in the region has to be restored. Through this agreement the following should be possible: (1) strict demarcation of parks, reserves and protection of habitats; (2) registration of weapons and wildlife, and control of poaching; (3) control of bush-forest burning; (4) research and surveys on which to base management, land-use planning, infrastructural development and regional co-operation. All these will lead to regional understanding, community-based development and permanent peace in the region.

Once peace in the region is restored, well-planned land-use management planning and community participation are vital. As Carpenter (1998) suggests, community-based bottom-up approaches for protection and conservation, will encourage popular participations rather than 'local partnership'. Top-down approaches may: (a) discourage local peoples and encourage outsider interests; (b) incur high costs for regional governments; and (c) aggravate conflicts between various interest groups, as well as between users and natural resources. Local participation and land-use management planning can: (a) help establish well-protected parks and well-planned settlements; (b) alleviate wildlife problems; (c) control bush-forest fires and illegal hunting; (d) provide sufficient forage and man-made watering sites, and health-care for wildlife considered to prevent foreseeable extinction.

Through community-based conservation and participation, the local people should be able to: (a) adapt to modern settlement sites; (b) participate in environmental education and/or training; (c) learn to respect and understand natural resources. Conservation planners in Africa in the past excluded local people from protected areas not only physically but also from participating in the planning and consultation processes. Many communities, therefore, were not and still are not interested in participating in wildlife conservation projects. The previous park projects such as Boma National Park on the Sudan side and Gambela National Park in the Ethiopian side, for example, were not implemented since these projects were established without the involvement of the local population, they interfered with the meat supply of the Anuak, and prevented the Murle and Nuer from grazing their animals and carrying out their traditional hunting practices (see also Blower, 1977).

Although Boma is a key area regarding wildlife conservation, the park was unmanaged and the wildlife population has been depleted (Blower, 1977). In the Gambela National Park alone, at least 85,000 people were resettled in 1996, which has badly affected wildlife habitats. The destruction of parks and reserves is a common phenomenon in many areas in the two countries. Even though there are 9 national parks, 11 wildlife sanctuaries, and 17 wildlife reserves in Ethiopia; and 6 national parks and 15 game reserves in the Sudan, none of them are effectively protected against poaching, deforestation or other illegal actions (Blower, 1977; EMO, 1988 and Leo Theuns, 1997).

Illegal action on the environment is mainly due to lack of community participation and land-use planning. The indigenous peoples are neither integrated into development activities, based on their needs, nor free from the effects of wars, deforestation and unplanned settlements/resettlements. The governments in the Region now have two choices: either the conservation of these high potential biodiversity areas and their remaining wildlife, or to continue the war, with destructive refugee settlements and resettlement schemes. If the indigenous peoples were supported to establish and implement wildlife conservation projects, they could utilise and manage wildlife resources (through their institutions) at low cost and could reduce poaching. Based on wildlife and biodiversity management techniques, eco-tourism can be designed for the Region as one of the world's natural heritages and most attractive eco-tourist regions in Africa. This would be a contribution to the global conservation efforts and could become a long-term self-sustaining conservation solution.

The proposed community-based eco-tourism is:
- an appropriate land-use option for the ecosystems in the region;
- a biodiversity conservation measure;
- a regional development strategy; and
- serves the development interests of both the Sudan and Ethiopia.

It may be one of the solutions to wildlife and biodiversity problems and should be considered as a sustainable and viable option to maintain the bio-physical and human environments. The following features make this suggestion highly attractive.
- There are many rivers, lakes and natural pools rich in aquatic life and plant species (Mengistu, 1995a & 1999).
- The Baro (Baro-Sobat-White Nile) is a navigable river for nearly 1400 km from Gambela town to Khartoum.
- The Region has a very rich natural biodiversity (Hillman, 1993; EVDSA, 1988 & 1990; TAMS, 1996);
- The indigenous peoples provide a rich cultural mosaic.
- The arable land is limited; since the soils in this flood plain are waterlogged, and the sandy soils contain acidic elements (Mengistu, 1996), many crops cannot be grown as easily as in many other parts of the two countries.
- The disease epidemiological situation is unfavourable both for humans and cattle.
- Some of the areas are prone to seasonal drought and floods (Caputo, 1993; EVDSA, 1988 & 1990; Mengistu, 1997a & 1999), which have become the main contributors to settlement/resettlement and agricultural development problems.

Due to environmental destruction, the long war, conflicts, population increase, settlement/resettlement concentration and land-use change, traditional riverbank farming, livestock rising, hunting, fishing and collecting activities have been difficult to maintain. In similar regions elsewhere, some authors (Allan,

1965; Kikula, 1997 & Mengistu, 1996) have suggested that under conditions of low population and scattered settlements, a land-use system approach would have an environmental conservation value in humid tropical regions where sandy soils are susceptible to erosion and vertisols suffer from water logging problems. The present dilemma is that the indigenous peoples in the study region have neither maintained the precious sustainable utilisation of natural resources nor have integrated themselves into other ways of life.

Further, the above-mentioned conservation strategies and wildlife utilisation methods can be interpreted also as wildlife ranching managements techniques, which is one of the basic requirements for successful eco-tourism. The term ranch is used in the context of well-planned, protected and managed parks, as well as reserves, and the utilisation of wildlife products for the benefit of the indigenous peoples. However, such kinds of management techniques require: (a) strong indigenous institutions; (b) well designed land-use planning; (c) introduction of artificial water-holes, forage and health-care; and (d) limited cropping and livestock activities as supplementary income for households. These wildlife ranching management techniques may: (a) be a solution to range land loss in Africa; (b) discourage poaching but encourage carefully planned hunting/slaughtering systems; (c) lead to the conservation of this rich diversity of wildlife and habitats; (d) protect livestock and crops - outside the parks and reserves - from being affected by wildlife; (e) control fire incidence, harvesting plant products and collecting honey; (f) attract eco-tourists world-wide; (g) provide the local people with employment opportunities, protein and adequate income; (h) help people to preserve old skills in danger of being lost; (i) pay for wildlife and biodiversity conservation, or provide a self-sustaining financial base for protected areas; (j) maintain a balance between wildlife and environment, and between species and habitats; (k) become one of the world's biodiversity and water storage regions; and (k) encourage regional and international co-operation rather than confrontation.

11.7 SUMMARY

Much of the wildlife and their natural habitats in the Region have been destroyed. This is largely owing to the massive refugee settlements and resettlement schemes and the large-scale mechanised farming in the limited environmentally vulnerable sites. Repeated wars and conflicts also adversely affect them. Regional biodiversity conservation strategies are required to safeguard both the natural and human ecosystems of the region.

If biodiversity were sustainable utilised, conserved and managed, different floristic periods would provide fruit for birds, Anubis baboons, and Grivet monkeys; and nutrients (from the great diversity of plants and numerous other organisms) to large wild animals. A regional biodiversity conservation strategy is a prerequisite if all aspects of sustainable land-use — land capability, wildlife and human ecosystems, in the region are to be restored. Unsustainable utilisation of natural resources and wildlife has led to migration, hunger and famine. As a result, automatic weapons are used for poaching as a survival mechanism.

As long as mismanagement of natural resources continues and conflicts are not resolved, more wildlife and biodiversity may become extinct locally in coming years. Since there is no systematic registration and recording system, it is important and urgent to monitor habitat conditions, understand the local communities' perceptions on conservation, introduce institutional capacity and awareness-building measures, undertake further research, surveys and mass education and/or training regarding environmental, technical and wildlife management, as well as understanding of wildlife and their relationships with other organisms.

12 CHAPTER 12: THE EFFECTS OF THE RESETTLEMENT SCHEMES ON HEALTH CONDITIONS WITH EMPHASIS ON THE SPATIAL SPREAD OF MALARIA

12.1 The Nature of Malaria

A few decades ago malaria was thought to be under control. Why is it then still a global problem, particularly in the tropical regions of the world? There are reasons to believe that the malaria problem is not caused only by the physical environmental factors but also by human-induced factors such as land-use changes and spontaneous/planned resettlement schemes.

Malaria is a disease caused by protozoan organisms called *Plasmodium. Falciparum, P. vivax, P. malariae* and *P. ovale*, which are refered to as malaria parasites or water-borne pathogens (Learmonth, 1977; Lysenko et al., 1969 and Prothero, 1965). The female mosquito of the genus Anopheles transmits the disease from one person to another. There are about 60 types of anopheline mosquitoes in the world. According to May (1961) these vectors are divided into 10 major regions. These include North America, Central America, East Africa, Central Africa, South Africa, Central Asia and South East Asia. The members of the *Anopheles gambiae* complex are the chief vectors in tropical Africa and Brazil. Malaria has its own geographical, ecological and environmental features in its life cycle. There are entomological, epidemiological, biotic, genetic and natural factors that affect spatial distribution of malaria and its impact on various human activities. It is the greatest contributor to inefficiency in the whole range of human activities (Stamp, 1964).

Malaria cases have increased and decreased through time and space in most parts of the world (Learmonth, 1977). Malaria and Africa are said to be almost synonymous. This disease is believed to have originated in tropical Africa during the Paleolithic and Mesolithic times. Through the effects of the agricultural revolution this disease was diffused into the Indus Valley, Mesopotamia, Southern China and the Nile Valley and then reached the Mediterranean, and then throughout the tropical and warm temperate regions of both old and new worlds (Bruce-Chwatt, 1965). The spatial spread of malaria appears to follow the diffusion of human settlement from Africa, the origin of man, to the rest of the world.

It is generally believed that malaria is a global, national, regional and local problem. It has no administrative boundary. Time and space play a key role in the interaction among the three main malaria components; namely, vector, parasite and host (see Figure 30). Mosquitoes take time and a conducive place to lay their eggs and pass the disease to another host. The parasite also requires time and space to complete the various stages of its life-cycle. In order to understand the geography of malaria and control the disease it is important to examine the relationships between *Anopheles* (vector), the *Plasmodium* (parasite) and the host (infected person); the physical factors (e.g. altitude, landforms, temperature, surface water, and vegetation); and the human factors (e.g. settlement patterns, population movement; human behaviour; development planning and land-use change).

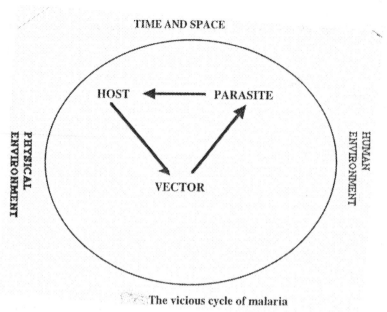

Figure 30. The vicious cycle of malaria

Without the presence of the host (humans), malaria transmission cannot take place. When a female mosquito vector bites a person to suck his/her blood (as its food) and that person is suffering from malaria, the malaria parasite can be transmitted to the next person that she bites (Colbourne, 1966).

12.2 The Global Spatial Spread of Malaria

The developed countries of today were affected by malaria in the past until it was controlled during the second half of the 19th century in Western Europe and the beginning of the 1950s in Eastern Europe (Learmonth, 1977 and May, 1961) as a result of the eradication campaigns. The disappearance of the disease was brought about by the following factors:
- Draining of water-logged areas and malaria-breeding grounds.
- Application of residual insecticides.
- The combination of anti-*Plasmodium* (parasite) treatment and anti-mosquito campaign; and
Improvements in nutrition, housing, hygiene and clothing (Learmonth, 1977 and May, 1961).

Today, malaria is a phenomenon of the developing countries but with global warming it could spread back to the developed countries within decades and become a public health problem for them again (Martin & Lefebvre, 1995). There were 140 countries or areas where malaria was endemic in 1955 (WHO, 1994), but the malaria cases had dropped from 280 million in the same year to 140 million by 1963 (Spensers & Thomas, 1969). Although malaria was once thought to have been brought under control in much of the world, in the 1950s 270 millions of the worlds population were already infected and about 1 to 2 million people used to die from malaria every year. Most of the increase in cases were from Africa (94 million clinical cases), South East Asia (5 to 10 million), Central and South America (1 to 2 mill.) and in Europe (about half a million) (Martin et al., 1995). About 40% of the malaria cases and 90 to 95% of malaria related deaths in the world are found in Africa. In Sub-Saharan Africa, where the transmission is high, malaria kills a million persons every year. Children under age of five and pregnant women constitute the most vulnerable groups.

There are two malarious geographical zones: endemic in the lower altitudes and epidemic in the higher altitudes. Africa is generally classified as having the highest levels of endemicity in the world. These malaria vulnerable zones were found up to 1000 m altitude with around 2000 mm rainfall per year, a minimum temperature of 19 to 20°C and savannah-forest vegetation. Endemic malaria decreases in areas that are located at less than 1500 m altitude, with below 19°C temperature and less than 1000mm rainfall per year, but the potential for epidemic outbreaks increases. The reason is that the lower the temperature the longer the parasite cycle. Although rainfall creates pools and streams as the breeding sites, high rainfall can also destroy these sites. Unexpected seasonal rainfall and high temperatures have brought epidemic malaria into the high altitudinal zones of Africa, such as Kenya, Ethiopia, Congo Democratic Republic and Zambia (WHO, 1992). For example, malaria increased by 501% in the previously malaria-free highland region in Rwanda in 1987 (Loevinsohn, 1994). This was due to increased ambient temperatures and unseasonal rainfall. This indicates that climatic change on a global level "is likely to modify malaria geography".

In the low latitudinal areas of Africa, between approximately 10°N to 10°S, conditions are highly favourable for the mosquito vectors to breed throughout the year. In the zones between 10 and 20°N and S where the rainfall is lower, malaria is more variable and unreliable both in amount and incidence, but between the equator and latitude 20°N and S there is no clear natural break in transmission; and therefore, malaria can occur at any time of the year in endemic form. This complex system of environments includes coastal swamp lake shores, islands, permanent and temporary rivers, desert fringes, peri-urban centres and the like. The land-use system includes such types as pastoral-nomadic, slash-and burn-cultivation, fishing and modern farming. Such activities have brought deforestation, population mobility, settlement and resettlement schemes, poorly-managed dams, the utilisation of wells, piped water and year-round irrigation (Gwadz, 1991). Increased incidence of the disease in modern settings has brought drug control also more available, but misuse of drugs has now led to large-scale drug resistance, both in the mosquito vectors and in the parasites. Large hydro-agricultural projects such as the Aswan Dam in Egypt, the Lake Volta in Ghana and similar projects elsewhere in the world are often blamed for upsurges in water-borne diseases. Although the highlands of Rwanda and Burundi are said to be free from malaria, 21,000 people were affected in the latter country in 1991 owing to the introduction of rice paddies in the highlands of that country (Johanson, 1992). In Madagascar malaria broke out in a formerly eradicated area and killed 25,000 people within a few months in 1988 (Prothero, 1965a or b?).

As long as mobility exists, highlanders can be exposed to malaria when travelling in the lowlands and then transmit the disease to previously malaria-free areas upon return to their home bases. The following are examples of groups that can introduce fresh malaria infections: seasonal labourers from Nigeria destined to the southern part of the country and to Ghana; pastoral-nomads going to and from Somalia, Sudan, Kenya and Ethiopia; population movements from the highlands of Rwanda and Burundi to the sisal-growing industry in Tanzania; the trading movements and exchange of commodities between and within the different environmental zones of Africa. Migrant workers from Thailand to the Thai-Cambodian border and to some villages in Burma and Vietnam and deforestation and resettlement in Brazil were shown to increase malaria cases in these countries 1990s. Areas, which were free from malaria in the 1960s in India, experienced malaria as the biggest health problem in the 1990s (Johanson, 1992 and Prothero, 1965).

Even though malaria control and eradication programmes have been introduced in many parts of the developing world, they often lack continuity and follow-up owing to physical constraints, poor management in irrigation and dam projects, political instability, and widespread poverty and drug resistance. Drug resistance means that the parasite develops resistance to quinine, chloroquine, tetracycline and other anti-malaria drugs (AAAS, 1991 and WHO, 1992).

The spatial distribution or spread of malaria as an environmental problem began to attract geographical research starting from the 1960s and 1970s (Learmonth, 1977; Lysenko et al., 1969; May, 1961 and Prothero, 1965). Recently, malaria distribution on the global level has been mapped by the WHO (Gilles, 1991).

12.3 The Spatial Spread of Malaria in Ethiopia

The limited studies on malaria in Ethiopia have focused mainly on the biology; behaviour and cycle of malaria vectors and parasites, and usually lack an interdisciplinary or geographical approach (see Mengistu, 1997b). As Wondatir et al. (1994) indicated the lack of adequate understanding of the epidemiology of malaria transmission has remained one of the major impediments to malaria control in Ethiopia. Although the National Programme conducted some studies in the 1980s for the Control of Malaria and other Vector-Borne Diseases under the Ministry of Health, none of these studies have yet been published or released.

Malaria (*woba or nidad* as it is called locally) is one of the most ancient diseases known in Ethiopia. Although the disease has been recognised for thousands of years, its scientific description and treatment were obscured by many magical and symbolic procedures.

In the 1930s and 1940s, the malariologists Covell (1957) and Melville et al. (1945) contributed to the knowledge of epidemiology of malaria by recording 42 *anopheline* species. This was latter supplemented by research under the National Malaria Control Programme. Of all mosquitoes in the country, about 60% were *Anopheles gambiae* s.l., 39% were *A. funestus* and *A. nili*, and the remaining 1% was other species (Negussie et al., 1988). The environment-malaria relationships are indicated in Table 10. Malaria has been one of the most widespread infectious diseases, particularly in the warm and moist lowland regions of the country having elevation of less than 1,500m and mean annual temperature varying from 20 to 30°C (Merid, 1958).

Ethiopia has various altitudinal regions and three geo-climatic zones. (Table 15). These include the *kola* or hot zone (46%), the *woyna dega* or temperate zone (46%) and the *dega* or cold zone (8%), i.e. the malaria free zone (Gilles, 1991). The average altitude in the *kola* is less than 1,500m; the mean temperature ranges between 20 to 30°C with 100 to 1,500mm of annual rainfall. In this region the malaria incidence varies from moderate to highly endemic. The altitude of the *woyna dega* zone is between 1,500 and 2,500m and the annual rainfall can reach 2,400 mm. The mean temperature is about 20°C and the malaria incidence varies from low endemicity to epidemic. In the *dega* zone, where the altitude is more than 2500 m and average temperatures are about 15°C, *Anopheles* mosquitoes cannot exist. Owing to insufficient water and moisture in the Danakil Depression, the Ogaden desert and similar regions, the presence of the *Anopheles* is weak. During the 1984 Resettlement Schemes thousands of people were mistakenly forced to move from the *woyna dega* and *dega* zones to the malaria prone zones in the humid western parts of the country.

Table 15. Environment and malaria relationships

Climatic Zone	Altitude (m.a.s.l.)	Mean annual temp. (°C)	Precipita-tion (mm)	Relative humidity %	Vegetation pattern	Population (%)	Incidence of malaria
Dega	>2000	15	1000-3000	20-30	Forest- savannah	37	Malaria free
Wayna dega	1500-2500	20	400-2400	30-40	Forest-savannah	45	Epidemic
Kolla	<1500	20-30	100-1200	60-70	Savannah-forest	18	Endemic

Epidemic or unstable malaria also occurs beyond its general geographical limit (e.g. above 1, 500-m elevation) within the highlands of Ethiopia. For example, 7,000 persons were killed by malaria in 1953 in the Dembia plain, north of Lake Tana, in Gondar Region that has an elevation of 1,800m. Similarly, more than 100 people were killed because of malaria in the same region between March and October of 1966. In the same year another incidence of malaria took place in Armachiho, in western Gondar.

In 1958 the highest altitudinal limit for malaria transmission was exceeded when malaria outbreaks were reported in the Debre Tabor area, between 1800 and 2,299 m, near Bahar Dar at 1,800m, the Zuquala plain and Akaki between 1,800 and 2200 m. Malaria also occurred between 1,400 and 2,000 m on the escarpment between Debre Sina (Shewa) and Adigrat (Tigray), and at Lake Haik (Wello) at 1,900 m altitude. The main reason for the 1958 epidemic was the abnormal weather conditions.

Hospital records indicate that in 1957 malaria killed more than 150,000 persons out of 3 million affected people. This outbreak led to the establishment of the Malaria Control Programme in 1959 as a joint effort between the Ethiopian Ministry of Health and the 'Point Four programme' of the USAID when an intensive DDT spraying operation was launched. In the 1960s and 1970s, several thousands of seasonal workers and pastoralists were affected in the Awash and Didesa Valleys, the Blue Nile, Baro-Akobo, Wabi-Shebele and Omo River Basins, Metema, Metekel, Arba Minch and southern Sidamo (Fontaine et al., 1961, Kloos, 1990, Negussie et al., 1988).

Even though the malaria problem was alleviated to some extent between the 1960s and 1970s, it is still the most difficult epidemiological and pharmacological challenge as well as the major cause of mortality and morbidity in many parts of the country. But due to some irrigation schemes in the Awash Valley, seasonal movement of the pastoralists and the spread of drug resistance in the areas bordering Somalia, Sudan and Kenya, the malaria cycle has been aggravated (Kloos, 1990).

The natural vegetation of the lowlands has been disturbed through free-grazing, unplanned settlements, introduction of commercial farms, and resettlement schemes, mainly in the Awash-Valley, Ogaden, Gambela, Setit Humera and Metekel. As a result, the biophysical environments were fundamentally disturbed affecting considerably those seasonal workers who had come from the malaria-free regions in the highlands (Assefa, 1991). On the other hand it is to be recalled that the DDT house-spraying campaigns, which were used widely throughout the country during the pre-1974 revolution period, were virtually terminated after 1974. This was perhaps due to the following reasons: (a) continued political unrest in the country; (b) anti-western government policies; (c) lack of malaria specialist and financial constraints; (d) forced and spontaneous population resettlements; and (e) land-use changes especially following the 1991-change of government and the associated regional policies.

In short, the establishments of the commercial farms in the 1950s and the state farms in the 1980s; the 1984 Resettlement Schemes and the subsequent Villagisation Programme together with the associated massive population movements were responsible for the large-scale increase of malaria cases in the country. The malaria cases increased from 43,545 between 1980 and 1984 to 234,592 cases between 1985 and 1989 (Assefa, 1991). Sivini (1986) estimated that the Resettlement Schemes in the whole of Ethiopia led to the loss of more people than those killed by the 1972 and 1984/85 famines.

Presently, malaria cases are increasing and the breeding sites are also expanding in most parts of the country, particularly in Gambela and other similar regions.

12.4 The Prevalence of Malaria in the Gambela Region and its Impact on the Settlement and Resettlement Processes.

The Gambela Region is a year-round endemic malaria transmission region (Krafsur, 1971 and Kloos, 1990). Table 16 gives the prevalence of malaria species in the Gambela Region.

Table 16. Prevalence of malaria species in Gambela, 1986-93

Year	Examined	Positive	P.Falciparum	Vivax	P.Malaria	Mix
1986	22669	7543	-	-	-	-
1987	107835	51479	-	-	-	-
1988	157134	71090	44352	27873	3	-
1989	202185	65489	58418	7589	82	-
1990	127296	30479	24099	6303	77	-
1991	12515	5148	4446	633	63	6
1992	20551	8286	6531	1670	76	9
1993	16813	7014	5291	1544	176	3

Note: - Data is not available.
Source: Data was obtained from the various health stations in Gambela.

The endemicity of malaria in the region is affected by the following inter-related physical and environmental factors, land-use and settlement patterns.

12.5 The Physical and Environmental Factors

Altitude: The prevalence and intensity of malaria follow the altitudinal and geomorphological features of the Region. The topographical diversity of the eastern part of the region, consisting of hills and valleys, is not conducive to larval development and has relatively low malaria endemicity. During the rainy season most larvae are washed away. As a result the activity of the vectors is weakened. Since the topography does not permit the creation of stagnant water pools the surface dries up as soon as the rains stop. This situation does not favour the development of malaria-carrying mosquitoes.

Most of the areas in the middle part of the Region are flat and wet for five to six months and dry up for the rest of the year. But these areas are associated with rivers, streams, ponds and swamps, all of which favour mosquito breading which results in the transmission of malaria throughout the year. The vast flat topography and hydrology of the western part, which is characterised by hot, swampy and flooded areas, is the most permanent malarious section of the region. .

Hydro-physical property: Since many of the rivers and streams drain from the east to the west cross the Gambela Region, the vast lowland area remains wet throughout the year. The flat topography and hydrology of the region is favourable for the mosquito vector to breed all year-round. Moreover, the clayey vertisols have pan like characteristics which allow them to maintain enough ponded water for a period long enough to allow the mosquito larvae to complete their development.

Climate: The Gambela Region is characterised by hot humid tropical climate. Thus, despite the fact that the Region is dry half of the year, owing to the availability of streams, ponds, lakes, pools and marshes it allows the mosquitoes to transmit malaria all the time. The available evidence indicates that the malaria incidence is mainly caused by high temperature and standing water rather than by high precipitation.

Vegetation: The rise and fall of the malaria incidence is also associated with the vegetation types found in the Gambela Region. Plants are generally valuable sources of natural chemical substances that are harmful to diseases and insects. For instance, the diverse and dense savannah vegetation found in the Gambela Region appears to contain natural anti-malaria substances. According to the belief of the indigenous people trees like *Terminalia axiflora* and *Azadirchita indica* have toxic substances which prevent flies and mosquitoes from entering the houses. The indigenous people also believe the milky juice of *Carica papaya* can protect people from malaria infection and other types of diseases (Mengistu, 1995a).

There is no widely accepted traditional cure for malaria in the Gambela Region Janssens et al. (1987) observed that the density of *A. gambiae* in Guinea and Sudan increased considerably with the degradation of the forest areas and thus was linked with human activities such as the expansion of the resettlement schemes.

Soils: The deforestation process has mainly occurred in the clay soil areas of central Gambela, which are now usually under cultivation by the resettlers. The clay soils are associated with water-logged areas, which seem favourable for the reproduction of the various vectors of infectious diseases (Mengistu, 1996 and Mengistu et al., 2001). Since the soil is always warm the maturation period of the mosquito is about 20 days. This allows the rapid reproduction of the disease-transmitting insects (EVDSA, 1988). The clay soils are capable of maintaining adequate ponded water for the mosquito larvae to complete their development.

12.6 Land-Use Changes and Epidemiology

As observed in the field, the present land-use changes, and particularly the destruction of the natural vegetation (which might act as anti-mosquito niches) and the introduction of new species seem to be one of the main causes for the epidemiological changes. According to the respondents, malaria cases before the 1970s and 1980s, were not as alarming as in the post-resettlement programme because: (a) the population was isolated from other malaria-prone people; (b) traditional anti-malaria or malaria protection measures were widely practices; (c) the population movement was confined within their own climatic region; (d) the non-immune highlanders, who migrated to Gambela, were very few and confined to the administrative centre; (e) they had an anti-malaria immunity system or haemoglobin; and (f) absence of man-made malaria breeding sites (such as dams, irrigation systems, etc.).

During the post-resettlement programme, the forest was destroyed for firewood, construction purposes and growing crops. As a result, the above mentioned land-use activities created change in the dynamics of transmission from seasonal to perennial. As Assefa (1993:348) pointed out, as a consequence of the resettlement programme, the formerly endemic or "stable malaria situation was replaced by explosive epidemics". During the fieldwork, 88% of the respondents believed that they were suffering from malaria and 12% from other water-related diseases. The main reasons for the high malaria and other disease cases detected during the 1980s was: (a) population increase; (b) the medical personals in the various Health Stations did not have incentives to provide proper medical-care; (c) the government did not allocate adequate financial assistance due to the war in north; (d) shortage of foreign exchange to import anti-malaria drugs; and (e) there was very limited aid as the country was isolated by the western donors.

The expansion of large-scale mechanised farms and settlement patterns not only led to deforestation and aggravate the natural flooding system and other determinants of the micro-climate, e.g. soil moisture but also created food shortage. When the food crops were no longer profitable, the land was converted to cash crop production like cotton. Although some resettlement farms were still used for maize (the major stable food crop in the region), its production declined by one-third in 1989 compared to the same period in 1988. All these destructive activities have brought deleterious effects on nutrition. The insufficient food created more people prone to suffer badly from malaria and other diseases because general poverty, improper housing and poor medical care already weakened them. The above-mentioned natural and man-made factors aggravated not only the malaria cases but also caused the non-malaria diseases (see Appendix 3).

12.7 The Health Stations in the Study Area

In 1990 there was one general hospital, located in Gambela town, one health centre, located at Itang and ten malaria control stations scattered in the settlement and resettlement sites. In general, the health stations lacked the basic equipment like, for example, a microscope to examine the blood smears for malaria, and drugs for malaria treatment. Necessary activities such as the monitoring of mosquito-breeding sites, house spraying with insecticides and house-to-house detection of diseases were rarely carried out.

The thatched-roofed health station also lacked proper sanitation and lights. As a result it was nearly impossible to protect the available scanty medical equipments and drugs from rain, insects, rodents and the like. Although in 1991 the thatched-roofs were replaced with corrugated iron-roofs, the overall conditions of the health station were still extremely unsatisfactory at the time when this study was being undertaken in 1996 (see Figure 31).

Figure 31. A Thatch-roofed health station (1989)

The health stations remained closed most of the time and the medical staff loitered around the towns. This was because they could not render their services effectively and regularly since they lacked the proper equipment and drugs, and above all incentives. In consequence very sick patients used to spend long hours in front of the closed health stations waiting hopelessly for medical services. In fact most of them had to die there unattended.

On the whole, health stations failed to provide proper services to the general public because of the following three major reasons: (a) The health stations were unable to make people aware of the need for protecting themselves from malaria, in particular, and report to the health stations for timely treatment; (b) The health stations did not possess the required medical facilities, trained personnel and drugs for primary health-care purposes; and (c) the badly needed transport services were not provided to the patients to go to the regional hospital.

12.8 SUMMARY

Various geographical factors, such as altitude, topography, surface water, climate, population movement, land-use changes, social and physical infrastructures, were found responsible for the spread of mosquito-borne malaria disease and other types of infectious diseases. The resettlement schemes neither understood the modern methods of malaria protection nor the traditional cures for malaria. The loss of a consider number of human lives could have been either avoided or minimised if the planners and policy-makers had consulted medical geographers, malariologists and entomologists before moving thousands of people from the malaria-free highlands to the malaria-prone and malaria-ridden lowland areas.

Ways ought to be sought to control or eradicate malaria and other diseases without at the same time affecting the human and physical environments. In order to cure malaria effectively a proper or right vaccine is badly needed.

Until such type of vaccine is introduced, the following malaria control and eradication measures ought to be taken:

Firstly the geography of the disease should be understood before any development project is launched in a malaria-prone region. Medical geographers and malaria specialists should provide adequate data to the planners and policy-makers concerning such aspects as the spatial distribution of the vectors, mosquito-breeding sites and the number of infected persons.

Secondly, the following requirement must be met: improved nutrition, water-supply and transport services; increased people's awareness regarding the malaria detection and prevention methods; house-spraying; and early diagnosis and prompt treatment of known malaria cases.

Thirdly, the following innovations should be assessed: introduction of anti-malaria fish species (e.g. *Gambusia)*, sterilisation of male malaria vectors; effective treatment of malaria cases; chemical larviciding; environmental control through draining of water-logged areas and other breeding sites. As recommended by Jaenson (1994) pyrethroid treated bed-nets, and detamethrin and lambreby (insecticide-treated) bed-nets are considered among the most important strategies in alleviating malaria transmission in the tropical environment. If nets are impregnated with permethrin every six months, the toxic contents can protect millions of people by killing, irritating and repelling the malaria vectors. These substances do not have detrimental effects on human beings; neither do they have the propensity to accumulate in the animal food chain.

Finally, it can be argued that some projects, like unplanned resettlement, can do more harms than good. For example, they can cause harm to the physical environment, humans, animal health, and crops. Moreover, they may involve high costs unless they are carefully planned and implemented. Furthermore, through the movement of people between neighbouring countries diseases such as malaria can be transmitted. Through the development of a community-based strategy, inter-sectoral, regional and international co-operation for effective malaria control methods can be undertaken.

13 Concluding Remarks

The policy-induced voluntary and involuntary resettlement schemes in many of developing countries have not helped to improve the well-being of the masses nor alleviated the land-use and environmental problems. Most of the resettlement projects have been designed on the basis of political motives and short-sighted political gains. Hence, they have operated as isolated entities, rather than as integrated development programmes. This has often led to land-use and ethnic-conflicts, deforestation, land degradation, damaging floods, food shortages and spread of diseases. Such environmentally damaging experiences, which have resulted from misconceived and misdirected policies, should provide important lessons to those countries that wish to embark upon workable or beneficial Resettlement Schemes or programmes.

It is unfortunate that Ethiopia has not succeeded in introducing sustainable rehabilitation schemes and rehabilitation programmes. Since the 1950s, various non-coherent and non-effective Resettlement Schemes have been practised in the country. These schemes have ended up in population displacement, disruption of the agrarian structure, the downfall of the socialist regime in 1991, and the biophysical and human environmental crises. These crises still continue, although in a diminished manner, owing to the sometimes-incompatible development priorities of the various ethnic groups, the structural readjustment policy, and political and social instability.

The results of the Gambela Region case study have demonstrated that the 1980s Resettlement Schemes ignored well-considered expert advice or recommendations as well the indigenous people's time- and experience-tested traditional knowledge regarding the value and conservation of their natural resources.

If appropriate planning had been undertaken and implemented, alternative land-use systems and conservation measures could have been adopted. Unfortunately failure to do this resulted in the following consequences:

- large-scale destruction of the traditional environmental management of the local natural resources;
- destruction of the biological biodiversity; and
- substantial human loss of life both in the sending and receiving regions.

Even though there were some gains in the form of social and physical infrastructures such as schools and roads, the Resettlement Schemes generally failed to consider the biophysical and human and environmental implications. Unfortunately, strong criticisms, especially those made by Western scholars, were labelled as against the socialist bases of the Resettlement Schemes without paying attention to the grave environmental issues facing the Region. It must be stressed, however, that since the ethnic-based regional political system was put in place in 1991, the regional environmental damage has not been repaired. In fact both those who left the resettlement areas and those who have remained there are still living under the most miserable conditions.

In order to mitigate the various environmental problems in the Gambela Region the following recommendations are being made:

- Give adequately appreciation to the indigenous peoples' traditional knowledge regarding their natural resources.
- Understand properly and implement new programmes, as far as possible, according to the needs and aspirations of the farmers' land-ownership system.
- Encourage the active participation of environmental scholars and other professionals in environmental management.
- Utilise actively and beneficially the Strategic Environmental Impact Assessment (SEIA)[1] technique in order to: be the basis of the future resettlement projects in the Gambela Region, develop peoples' awareness of the changes in the environment and their implications, develop capacity and awareness building measures, individual and group responsibilities; and better empowerment of women, develop environmentally conscious societies who act collectively and think decisively, encourage stability, peace and regional security through the regional development process and good governance and develop agrarian-based rural towns to stem the large-scale migration of the rural people to the urban areas.
- come up with appropriate sustainable technological package, land-use planning and effective protection and preservation of biodiversity as well as sustainable utilisation of wildlife and its habitats as viable land-use options, which can contribute to the recovery, maintenance, and improvement of the region's ecosystems.

As long as land-use is not properly planned (based on land suitability, land capability and the needs of the peoples), the deteriorated environment can not be rehabilitated. Since the topography, hydro-geology and temperature are suitable, Gambela can supply high quality and quantity of timbers, grasses (*Penisenum purpureum* and *Panicum maximum*, useful for manufacturing industries and to feed animals), variety of wildlife, as well as various types of energy all of which are needed by the surrounding highland regions. If the farmers in the crop producing areas in the highlands are supplied with proper inputs, they can also produce high quality and quantity of crops and livestock products, which are not available in the Gambela region. These are the bases for regional co-operation and understanding, (re)settlement integration and improvement of the natural and human ecosystems.

Finally, the study has revealed succinctly that the human-induced environmental damage, in particular, is characteristic of developing countries like Ethiopia. In consequence, those scholars who are interested in conducting research on the impact of both the physical and human environments should be engaged vigorously in pursuing such studies, as sustainable economic development in developing countries is very closely associated with sustainable environmental development.

---

[1]) In order to achieve environmentally sustainable (re)settlement project, a good SEIA on the programme is a tool for (re)settlement planners and decision-makers. SEIA may cover such as biophysical, economic and socio-cultural impact analysis, as well as risk and technological assessment.

14 APPENDICES

14.1 Appendix 1: The geology of the Gambela Region

The major geological features of the Gambela/Abobo Region are briefly described below (See also Chapter 6 and EVDSA, 1988):

Rock outcrops occur in the eastern and northern parts of the sub-region and submerges westward and south-westward.

The soil materials found at the feet of the gentle slopes appear to have been formed from the basaltic lava flows from non-fragmented Oligocene-quaternary and deluvial, colluvial and elluvial fragments.

The Pliocene-lower and Pleistocene deluvial-elluvial sediments mostly occur in the hilly and mountainous zones and are mostly represented by sandy loams and loams with some ferruginous conglomerate layers in some localities.

The early and middle Pleistocene deluvial-proluvial formation is found mixed with the other geological materials in the foothills of the sub-region. Sands, loamy sands and loams with gravels and pebbles are widespread along the Alwero formation whereas the deluvial-proluvial deposits overlie the Gilo formation. The materials seem to be the remnants from the basaltic lava flows along the eastern parts of the mountainsides towards the west.

The upper Pleistocene lacustrine alluvial formation occurs mainly between the Itang and Gambela towns, and between the Abobo and Uwela plains. The depression is filled with what is called the Alwero sandstone and is water-bearing. The parent materials consist of kaolinized sandstones and iron-bearing materials.

Modern lacustrine-alluvial sediments or deposits are found in the swampy areas and rivers in the west of the sub-region. The sediment has accumulated from the rivers that flow from the higher altitude areas to the east. The soil type in this area is clayey which shows surface cracks during the dry season. Cracking seems to have a big impact on the translocation of materials. It influences soil structure, plant rooting system and ground water environment.

Modern alluvial deposits cover the eastern and central parts of the sub-region and occur mainly along the Alwero and Gilo rivers where they are known as the Alwero, Teppi and Gilo formations. The Gilo formation occurred during the Palaeocene-Oligocene age and covers the depressions in the crystalline basement having a thickness of 5–600 meters. The north-westerly plunging depression of the basement lies in the lower plain and the composition of the deposits includes arkose feldspar (rich sandstone) and calcicretes mixed with quartz-pebbles. The arkose contains 15% clay-iron materials, which are covered by calcareous cement, which are later replaced by aleurolites sand-clay. This indicates that the flow of basaltic lava that was transported from the upper altitude covered the Gilo sandstone. The soils of this area vary from clayey-loamy to loamy sands.

The general drainage pattern of the sub-region is controlled by the east-west and north-south trending geological structures. The Gog basalts are one of the water-bearing rocks and the Abobo water bearing formation (i.e. artesian aquifer composed of Pliocene deposits) is one of the most reliable sources of water in the region. Because of the problems of water percolation, the ground water is shallow in the swampy areas and deep in the moderately permeable soils in the foothills of the eastern and central parts of the sub- region.

14.2 Appendix 2: Soil types of the Gambela Region

The nine soil types and their respective characteristics are presented in the following Table (Table 17). See also Figure 15 in Chapter 6.

Table 17. A summary of soil formation factors, approximate elevation divisions, soil vegetation types and hydrological characteristics in the study region

Soil Types	Soil Characteristics	Elevation and Topography	Parent Material	Climate
Nitosols	Laterised, humus, heavy clay, rich in base, Thick and well aggregated, low EC, acidic, Available P & K are mobile, sufficient N.	Steep slop, rolling surface, and 1000-2000 m a.s.l.	Basalt and other Quaternary deposits.	>1200 mm annual rainfall, moderate temperature and good moisture.
Litosols	Immature brown soils, low humus, low fertility and lateritic pan, skeletal soils in combination with terrigenous tropical soils, rich in loams.	Formed under complicated topography, 800-1000 m a.s.l.	Loose rock	Moderate temperature.
Ferralsols	Brownish-red, well drained, thick, deep surface cracking, rich in clays, loams and humus, mobile P & K, sufficient N, Ca, EC, slightly alkaline and Fe-Mn concretion.	600-800 m a.s.l.	Quaternary deposits, iron cemented quartz, Fe-Mn concretions.	1100 mm mean annual precipitation and ambient temperature.
Pelllic Vertisols	Deep-black vertisols, heavy texture, deep cracking, moderate EC, low humus, mobile P & K, Ca, Mg as exchangeable cations, slightly alkaline and nutrient deficient.	400-500 m a.s.l.	Lacustrine-alluvial clay.	Rainfall and floods provide moisture for soil materials.

Glay Vertisols	Alluvial-meadow bog soils, heavy texture, high humus and EC, acidic, mobile P & K, fine silt, deep surface cracking, Fe-Mn concretion.	Flat plain, old riverbeds and hollows, 550-560 m a.s.l.	Ancient deltaic deposits, riverbed alluvial sands.	800-900 mm annual precipitation, tropical ambient temperature.
Chromic Vertisols	Sandy loams, poorly aggregated silty profiles, high humus content, reddish brown, clayey, surface compaction, Fe-Mn concretion.	Undulating plain, 500-550 m a.s.l.	Alluvial loams and sandy loams.	4-7 dry months and 1000 mm mean annual precipitation.
Fluvisols	Sands, sandy loams, meadow, compacted fluvisols, deep gleyic, gley, heavy silt and clay texture, high EC and humus mobile P & K, slightly acidic, Ca & Mn exchangeable cations.	Old riverbeds, flat land, 500-550 m a.s.l.	Alluvial clays, loams and sandy loams.	950 mm annual precipitation.
Forest Cambisols	Low humus, heavy texture, brown, dark-brown, high clay and humus content, low EC, Fe-Mn content.	Denudation-aggradation landforms, 500-600 m a.s.l.	Loose rock, basalt weathering products, grains and gravel of quartz and feldspar.	950 mm annual precipitation and tropical ambient temperature.
Savannah Cambisoles	Shallow soils, low humus, heavy-light texture, compact, Fe-Mn concretion, low EC and low nutrient supply.	Forest land, roll and ridges, 500-520 m a.s.l.	Alluvial deposits.	950 mm annual precipitation.

Table continued (additional columns)

Soil Types	Hydrology	Vegetation	Land-use and Land Suitability	Land Potential
Nitosols	Ground water is deeper than 200 m but does not influence soil formation.	Tropical rain forest or evergreen forest.	Arable land needs organic fertilisers.	Erosion on steep slope, denudation on plains and river valleys.
Litosols	Low water table and availability of moisture depends on floods and rainfall.	Evergreen and deciduous tropical rain forest.	Only a small area of land can be used for grazing but good for forest.	Less suitable for agriculture because of leaching.
Ferralsols	Fresh ground water (20 m deep).	Deciduous tropical forest, savannah grass and high in leaf litter decay products.	Partly arable land which requires organic and inorganic fertilisers.	High leaching and water erosion in gully forms.
Pelllic Vertisols	Old and small rivers get lost in swampy areas.	Savannah grasses with different tree species.	Requires inputs due to waterlogged depression.	Lateral and sheet erosion in riverbeds.
Glay Vertisols	Swampy surface is connected with the river and ground water.	High grass savannah with low trees.	This swampy area is unstable for agricultural activities.	High leaching.
Chromic Vertisols	>20-m ground water depth, water logging in depressions associated with rainfall.	High grass savannah with scattered trees.	Unsuitable for agricultural activities due to physical characteristics.	Leaching occurs.
Fluvisols	Meanders, ox-box lakes and ancient delta origin, ground water are connected with river flow.	Deciduous low trees and savannah grass.	Suitable for sprinkler irrigation.	Erosion on river flood plains.
Forest Cambisols	Drained and low water percolation areas.	Evergreen and deciduous tropical forest	Need organic and inorganic fertilisers.	Erosion in combination with gullies.
Savannah Cambisols	Poorly drained areas and 20 m ground water depth.	Deciduous forest and grass savannah.	Requires irrigation, organic and inorganic fertilisers.	Leaching occurs.

Note: The Table is a summary of the various literature cited in the text and from my first hand data collected from the study region.

The Nitosols (red laterised soils) are well-developed soils formed from intermediate to basic parent materials that are found in most of the East African landscape, including the Gambela Region. These Nitosols make well-drained loamy soils that have good porosity in the soil solution, Al toxicity, high moisture storage capacity, and high cation exchange capacity content (Driessen et al., 1989). The eutric nitosols, which are fertile red soils, are mainly found on the well drained gently undulating terrain located both in Dumbong and Ukuna Kijang areas. It is confirmed that the Nitosols occur in association with Lithosols and have good physical properties such as high infiltration capacities, which allow for deep penetration of roots. These soils are well developed under the vegetation types ranging from forest and woodland to grassland.

The Lithosols, which are immature tropical brown soils are found in the loose rock environment. These soils are generally classified as skeletal soils, which are found in association with Feruginous tropical red soils and the brown savannah soils. They are "formed upon the bedrock eluvium albic E horizon, especially in the profile of the solodic savannah, which has light texture in its upper part and heavy texture in its lower part" (FAO-UNESCO, 1971). These soils are found in the complicated topographic conditions of Abobo, which stretch from northeast to southeast on the folded land surface and are characterised by good moisture retention and moderate temperature. Geomorphologically these soils are formed above loose rocks such as gneisses and granites. The elluvial loams represent the parent materials but the soil properties are not yet developed owing to the unfavourable soil forming environments.

The Ferralsols (the ferruginous tropical soils) are derived from the basaltic rocks, which provide alluvial sediments in the lower parts of Abobo and have ferralistic pans. The Ferralsols occupy the central part of Abobo and are confined to the humid tropical climatic zone. They are strongly weathered, have clayey content and relatively good physical properties. The vegetation type in this area includes semi-deciduous forest and the savannah and therefore gives the soil high humus content.

The Pellic Vertisols are typical tropical black soils. These are one of the sub-types of the verticals and cover most of the depressions in the permanent swampy areas north of Fekadi up to the border of the Perpengo area. In the temporary swampy areas the soils become hard during the dry season, which creates problems for ploughing. Various types of the flat-bottomed depressions such as old riverbeds disappear in the swampy areas and aggravate the flat topography. These soils have a gleyification character at different depths. Since a mantle of heavy impervious clay separates the topsoil from the ground water the soil moisture comes only from rainfall and floods. Compaction, heavy texture, severe dehydration, high calcium and manganese content, low mobile P and K, low humus content and low exchangeable sodium were observed. The Pellic vertisols seem to have low kaolinite and high smectite content. Since this area is poorly drained, it requires high inputs for agricultural development.

The Gley Vertisols (the tropical black soils) occur in the temporary and permanent swampy areas. The parent materials seem to be derived from riverbed alluvium; sandy loam, sand and new soils accumulated every year owing to the deposition of clay and silt by water. Waterlogged depressions create difficulties for new land- use in view of the poor conditions for roots and soil fauna.

The Gley Vertisols mainly cover the depression of the western part of Fekadi up to the border of Itang. This area receives water from rain and flood. The soil materials are hard when dry and sticky when wet. The soil texture in the waterlogged area varies from heavy clay to light clay. The swampy area serves as an efficient natural nutrient trap and helps to form refugee for plant and animal species.

The Chromic Vertisols (tropical black soils) are located in western and southern Abobo. These soils, which are classified as lateritic and proluvial sub-types, have dark and brown colour and are found bordering the Fluvisols and Phaeozems. They are derived from young alluvial deposits and have deep, very dark grey to black clay content. The surface texture is clayey whereas above the 50 cm level coarse textural layers occur (US AID and Ministry of Agriculture, 1976). With the exception of some soils in some areas, the upper part of these soils is poorly aggregated. The soils with high clay content show physical cracking throughout the dry season, but contain adequate supplies of humus and nutrients. It is also observed that in the areas where the sodium content is high the humus horizon is also high (EVDSA, 1988).

The Fluvisols (alluvial soils) have two sub-types: meadow and laminated ones which have compaction characteristics: These soils are developed from recent alluvial deposits which receive fresh materials at regular intervals (FAO-UNESCO, 1971). The Fluvisols are situated in the alluvial valley environment and in the main flooded areas. They are mainly found in association with the Chromic Vertisols. These soils are also classified as the Utric Fluvisols, the alluvial Soddy soils, or the Alluvial Medeow soils. They are saturated with water owing to floods during certain periods of the year. They have a heavy silt-clay texture. Their humus horizons are rich in clay and fine silt; and their particle contents measure ranging from less than 0.01 mm to 0.5 mm.

The Forest Cambisols (immature siallitic brown soils) occur together with the Ferralsols (Driessen et al. 1989). In the Abobo Sub-Region these soils have internal drainage, good water-holding capacity, high CEC, high humic content and are both intensively and poorly drained. The Forest Cambisols are said to be highly humic soils resulting from clay and loams. They are one of the most productive soils encountered in the Sub-Region.

The Savannah Cambisols (solodic sialitic brown soils) occupy a small area in northwestern part of Abobo. They are found on the gently undulating terrain bordering the Gley and Chromic Vertisols. They are characterised by a combination of the solodic siallitic and savannah soils and has partly Eutric and partly Dystic characteristics. These soils are also known as bleached meadow. Low humus, insufficient supply of nutrients, nearly neutral reaction, and light and heavy texture are the main characteristic features of these soils. This might be the main reason why neither traditional nor modern farming system has been introduced. Therefore, inorganic and organic fertilisers are required in order to make this soil-area productive.

14.3 Appendix 3. The Prevalence of Non-Malaria Diseases and their Impact on the Settlement and Resettlement Processes. See Chapter 12.

The part had identified environmentally related non-malaria diseases in the Gambela Region. The symptoms and epidemiological features of the selected disease categories include *Trypanosomiasis; Yellow Fever; Intestinal Parasites; Onchocerciasis; Helminotoses; Diarrhoea; Schistosomiases* and

Kala-Aazr (Leishmaniasis). Among theses diseases the more common ones are discussed at some length. These include trypanosomiasis, yellow fever, intestinal parasites and onchacerciasis.

14.3.1 Trypanosomiasis

Trypanosomiasis is a vector of the tsetse fly and the humid tropical Africa is the endemic home. Hoare (cited by Merid, 1988) and Stamp (1964) contended that the *Glossina palpalis* transmit *T. gambiense* which causes sleeping sickness in humans and the fly known as the *Glossina marsitans* causes the *Rhodesiense* form of sleeping sickens to animals. The WHO (1979) studies showed that the *T. gambiense* type was located in Africa between 15° N and 18° S of the equator extending from Lake Victoria to the coastal regions of Senegal, Angola and the Democratic Republic of Congo. The *T. rhodesiense* type extends from Mozambique, Malawi and Zimbabwe, Zambia to Tanzania, Kenya and Ethiopia. In 1979 alone, about 35 million Africans were exposed to this disease.

In Ethiopia Kefa, Gamo Gofa, Sidamo, Shewa and Gojam, the Glossina fly type often infests Welega and Illubabor. In accordance with the Central Statistical Authority of Ethiopia (1981), six Glossina species were found along the Baro, Omo and Blue Nile River Basins, but the *T. gambiense* type is largely confined to the forest areas found in the eastern part of the Region and along the major rivers of Akobo, Gilo and Baro. The most seriously affected people by the disease in the Region are the Anuaks. The Nuers are not affected by this disease as they reside beyond the fly-belt zone (Merid, 1988).

Wild animals are generally believed to have high tolerance for animal *Trypanosomiasis*. In view of this the Anuaks follow the ecological system and use wild animals for meat and skin as well as for growing cereals and stable food. After the launching of the Resettlement Schemes in the Region cattle were introduced. But they were exposed to the disease and most of them did not survive. For example in the Ukuna Kijang resettlement sites the 40 heads of cattle which were brought in 1990 died in 1991.

14.3.2 Yellow fever

The yellow fever is mosquito-borne disease, which is confined, to the West Coast of Africa and across Sub-Saharan Africa including the Sudan, Angola and Ethiopia. These regions are inhabited by the vectors belonging to the subgenus *Stegonyia* of the genus *Aedes* (Brown, 1977 and Spencer, 1973). The agents of transmission are forest monkeys and certain rodents. Since the disease can breed on water reservoir, water jugs and the like it is active both in the rainy and dry seasons (Merid, 1988 and EVDSA, 1988). It is also believed that plants such as palms and banana, which hold water between the stems, can be hosts to the yellow fever (Stamp, 1964).

In 1984, 5.5 million people, who resided in south-western Ethiopia, were infested by the rural type yellow fever. The most affected areas were Assosa, and the Omo and Didesa River Valleys (Merid, 1988), Lake Abaya and the Akobo River (Gambela).

14.3.3 Intestine parasites

Intestinal protozoans are single-celled living things, which are one of the main environmentally induced diseases and are mostly found in the tropics. Among the six species, only *Entamoeha. histolytica* is a pathogenic to humans. This is the agent of the amoeba disease, which affects people in the country (Tesfa-Michael, 1988). Out of the 171 patients who visited the Gambela hospital in 1986 the amoeba disease affected one percent. The main causes of this disease were lack of latrines and health education, shortage of clean water inadequate shelters or houses and general poverty.

14.3.4 Onchocerciasis

Onchocerciasis or river blindness is caused by a parasitic worm known as *Onchocerca volvulus,* which is transmitted to many people by multiple bites of the infected black flies. The worm releases embryos into the skin which provoke itching which in turn invades the eye that leads to river blindness. Like the malaria disease the *Onchocerciasis* is a result of the links among the agent, vector and host. It is also influenced by the physical and human environmental factors.

Entomological investigations in Ethiopia show that the *Simuium damnosum and Simulum woodi ethiopiense* have been identified as the principal vectors of *Onchocerciasis*. The disease is endemic in southwestern regions of the country covering an area of 132, 000-km^2 including the Gambela Region. Nevertheless, it is not known as to how many people are affected by this disease. Similarly, the spread of this disease within the Gambela Region is also not known. But in general, of the total *onchocerciasis* patients who visited the Gambela hospital between 1980 and 1984 about one third came from the Illubabor Administrative Region, which included the Gambela Region. Even though the data on this disease are scanty, the non-planned and planned resettlement included large-scale mechanised farms which had increased the transmission of this disease (Zein, 1988).

An attempt has been made to compare the malaria patients with the patients of the non-malaria patients for the year 1991. The laboratory results in the Gambela hospital showed that 43% of the total patients who visited the hospital in that year were malaria cases. Most of these were those who lived in and around the Gambela town. But those who lived in distant places (i.e. more than 10 km.) were not examined in the hospital owing to the physical distance barrier, lack of transportation, and the patients from the resettlement sites were not permitted to leave their places.

15 REFERENCES[2]

AAAS (American Association for the Advancement of Science) (1991): Malaria and Development in Africa, Washington D.C: 5-40.

Abdul Hamid Bedri (1988): Awash (re)settlement Programme. Paper presented at the IDR (AAU). Workshop on Famine and (re)settlement in Ethiopia (unpublished), Addis Ababa.

Abir, M. (1980): Ethiopia and the Red Sea, Frank Class and Cousary Ltd, London.

Aggrey-Mensah, W. (1988): Degradation of the Ethiopian highlands and actions to combat it, soil and economic implication, costs and benefits. Working Paper 12. Ethiopian Highland Reclamation Study, Ministry of Agriculture/FAO, Addis Ababa.

Allan, W. (1965): The African Husbandman, Heineman, London.

Alemayehu Lirenso (1989): Villagisation and agricultural production in Ethiopia: A case study of two regions, IDR Research Report 37, Addis Ababa University.

Alemeida, de A. (1954): The History of Ethiopia or Abyssinia, 1628. In: Beckingham, C.F. et al. (eds.): Some records of Ethiopia, 1593-1646, Series 2 (107): 3-96, London.

Asmerom Legesse (1973): Gada, the Free Press, New York.

Assefa Mehiretu (1964): The changing landscape of the Wanji plain (B.A. Thesis). Department of Geography, HSIU, Addis Ababa.

Assefa Mehiretu (1986): Towards a framework for spatial resolution of the structural polarity in African Development. Economic Geography, vol. 62 (1):30-51.

Assefa Negash (1991): Population migration and malaria transmission in Ethiopia. In: AAAS (ed.): Malaria and Development in Africa, Washington D.C:181-89.

Assefa Negash (1997): Ethnic regionalization and its ramifications on health: A study of malaria epidemics in Ethiopia. Ethiopian Register: 22-8.

Assefa Nega Tulu (1989): Malaria in Ethiopia, its changing epidemiology and the potential role alternative diagnostic and control methods, Master's Thesis. London School of Hygiene and Tropical Medicine.

Assefa Nega Tulu (1993): Malaria. In: Kloos, Helmut and Zein Ahmed (1993): The ecology of health and disease in Ethiopia. Western Press (Boulder, San Fransisco, Oxford).

Azene Bekele (1993): Useful Trees and shrubs for Ethiopia. SIDA's Regional Soil Conservaton Unit, Nairobi.

Bahru Zewde (1970): A biography of Dezamach Jote, Tulu Aba Iggu (1855-1941): B.A. Thesis, Department of History, Haile Selassie I University.

Bahru Zewde (1982): An overview and assessmment of Gambela trade (1904-1935). East Africa History Conference Proceeding, Adama Hotel, Nazreth, Ethiopia, the Institute of Ethiopian Studies (AAU), December 15-20: 165-91.

Bahru Zewde (11991): A history of modern Ethiopia 1855-1974. James Curry, London.

Baker, J.N.L. (1963): The history of geography, Oxford Basil Blackwell.

Barbour, K.M. (1961): The republic of Sudan, regional geography, University of London Press.

Birkeland, P. W. S. (1984): Soils and geomorphology, New York.

---

[2]) Ethiopian authors are listed alphabetically by first name.

Blower, J.H. (1977): Wildlife conservation and management in the southern Sudan (UNDP/FAO), Rome.

Bodvall, G. (1959): Bodland i norra Hälsingland, studier i utmarksodlingars roll för den permanenta bosättningens expansion fram till 1850. Geographica 36. Uppsala Appelbergs AB.

Bray, R. H. & Kurtz, L.T. (1945): Determination of total, organic and available forms of phosphorus in soils. Soil Science 59: 39-45.

Brown, L.A. & Kevin, R.C. (1971): Empirical regularities in the diffusion of innovation. Annals of the Association of American Geography 61: 511-59.

Bruce-Chwatt, L.J. (1965): Paleogenesis and paleo-epidemiology of primate malaria. Bulletin WHO 32 (3):363-87.

Bylund, E. (ed) (1974): Ecological problems of the circumpolar area, Luleå. Norrbotton 17.

Bylund, E. (1960): Theoretical considerations regarding the distribution of settlement in inner Northern Sweden. Geografiska Annaler, vol. 42B: 225-31.

Caputo, R. (1993): Tragedy stalks the Horn of Africa, National Geographic Society 184 (2): 87-122.

Carpenter, J.F. (1988): Internally motivated development projects: a potential tool for biodiveresity conservation outside and protected areas. AMBIO 27 (3): 211-16.

Chambers, R. (1969): Settlement schemes in tropical Africa. A study of organizations and development. Rutledge and Kegan Poul, London.

Chisholm, M. (1962): Rural settlement and land-use. London, Hutchinson.

Chisholm, M. (1979): Rural settlement and land-use. An essay in location, Third Edition, London, Hutchinson.

Christaller, W. (1966): Central places in Southern Germany. Engle wood Cliffs, Prentice-Hall.

Clarke, J. (1987): Ethiopia's campaign against famine, London.

Clark, C. (1987): Deforestation and floods. Environmental Conservation 14 (1): 67-9.

Clout, H. (1979): Rural settlement. Progress in Human Geography, vol. 3 (3): 417-24.

Cohen, J.M. & Isaksson, N.I. (1987): Villagisation in the Arsi region of Ethiopia. Rural Development Studies 19, Swedish University of Agricultural Sciences.

Colbourne, M. (1966): Malaria in Africa, Oxford University Press, London.

Conway, D., Krol, M., Alcamo, J. & Holme, M. (1996): Future availability of water in Egypt: the interaction of global, regional and basin-scale driving forces in the Nile basin. AMBIO 25 (5): 336-42.

Coulson, A. (1982): Tanzania, a political economy, Oxford, Clarendon Press.

Covell, J. (1957): Malaria in Ethiopia. Journal of Tropical Medical Hygen 60: 70-16.

CSO (Central Statistical Office) (1988): Statistical Abstract, Addis Ababa.

Dacey, M.F. (1962): Analysis of central place and point patterns by nearest neighbour methods. Proceedings of the IGU Symposium in Urban Geography. A publication in Lund Studies in Geography B 24:55-75.

Dagew Eshetu (1986): RRC, rehabilitation programme, RRC, Addis Ababa,

Daniel Gamachu (1983): Peripheral Ethiopia, a look at the marginal zones of the country. Paper presented on regional planning and development in Ethiopia, 14th and 17th of April, Ambo Ethiopia.

Dansereau, P. (1957): Biogeography: an ecological perspective, New York.

Daubennire, A. C. H. (1968): Ecology of fire in grassland. Advances in Ecological Research 5: 209-66.

De Blij, H.J. & Muller, P.O. (1988): Geography, regions and concepts, Fifth Edition, USA.

Dejene Aredo (1990): The time-space dimension of the Villagisation programme in Ethiopia. Dortmund: Fachgebiet Geographische Grundlagen der Raumplaning, Universität Dortmund, Arbeitspapiere 8.

Despois, J. & Raynal, K. (1967): Geographie de l'Afrique du Nord-Ouest, Payot, Paris.

Dessalegn Rahmato (2003): Resettlement in Ethiopia. The tragedy of population relocation in the 1980s. Forum for Social Studies, Addis Ababa, June.

Detroit Free Press (1991): Operation Moses and Operation Solomon 1/71.

Driessen, P.M. & Judal, R. (eds.) (1989): Lecture notes on the geography, formation, properties and use of the major soils of the World. Agricultural University, Waggningen, Katholieke Universiteit Leuven.

Duncan, P. (ed.) (1992): Zebras, asses, horses and an action plan for the conservation of wild equids. IUCN, Gland.

Duncan, F. & Brown, M.J. (1995): Edaphics and fire. An interpretative ecology of lowland forest vegetation on granite in Northeast Tasmania. Proceedings of the Linnean Society of New South Wales 115: 45-60.

Edward, U. (1977): The von Thunen principle and agriculture zonization in Colonial Mexico. Journal of Historical Geography 3: 123-33.

Edwards, S., Mesfin Tadesse, Sebsebe Demissew and Hedberg, I. (2000): Flora of Ethiopia & Eritrea, volume 2, part 1: Magnoliaceae to Flacourtiaceae. Addis Ababa, Ethiopia and Uppsala, Sweden.

Ellman, A. (1972): An agricultural and socio-economic survey of south Sudan refugee Settlements and surrounding areas in Gambela *Awraja*, Addis Ababa (IAR).

Ethiopian Government (1967): First Five-Year Development Plan (1957-61). Addis Ababa, Planning Commission.

EMO (Ethiopian Mapping Organisation) (1978): topographic map, scale: 1: 200000, sheet 20 and series 2201, Addis Ababa.

ENA (Ethiopian National Atlas) (1988): Ethiopian Mapping Agency, Addis Ababa.

Evans-Pritchard, E.E. (1972): The Nuer, Fifth Edition, USA.

EVDSA (1988): Master plan of the integrated utilisation of the water and land resources of the Gambela Plain, vol. 1-6, Addis Ababa.

EVDSA (1990): Geomorphology, geology and hydrology, vol. 15: Annex 2-3, Addis Ababa.

FAO-UNESCO (1971): Soil map of the world, vol.1, Scale 1: 5000000, UNESCO, Paris.

FAO (1986): Ethiopian Highland Reclamation Study, vol., Rome.

Farmer, B.H. (1974): Agricultural Colonization in India since Independence, London.

Fearnside, P.M. (1986): Human Carrying Capacity of the Brazilian Rainforest, New York, USA, Colombia University Press.

FGE (Federal Government of Ethiopia) (1997): Environmental Policy. Environmental Protection Authority in collaboration with Ministry of Economic Development and Co-operation. Addis Ababa, 2 April.

Fontaine, R.E., Najjar, A.E. & Prince, J.S. (1961): The 1958 Malaria Epidemic in Ethiopia. Am. J. Trop. Med. Hyg. 10: 795-803.

Foster, B.E. (1989): The Rwandese Refugees in Uganda. In: Hjort, A. et al. (ed.), Ecology and Politics, SIAS: 145-55.

Friis, I. (1992): Forests and Forest Trees of Northeast Tropical Africa: Their Naural Habitats and Distribution Patterns in Ethiopia, Djibouti and Somalia. Her Majesty's Stationary Office, London.

Friis, I., Rasmussen, F.N. & Volleson, K (1982): Studies in the flora and Vegetation of Southwest Ethiopia. Opera Botanica 63: 1-70.

Gamble, C. (1978): Människan kolonisera jorden. Forskning och framsteg 7: 1-6. Tryckindustri AB, Solna (Stockholm).

Gerrard, A.J. (1981): Soils and Landforms, an Integration of Geomorphology and Pedology, George Allen & UNWIN, London.

Gibbons, A. (1997): Human Evolution, Sciences, vol. 278 (31): 804-05.

Gilles, H.M. (1991): Management of Severe and Complicated Malaria, WHO, Geneva.

Gouin, P. (1972): Seismic Zoning in Ethiopia, Bulletin of the Geophysical Observatory 17, Addis Ababa.

Gol'ts, G.A. (1986): Development Stages, Structural Level and Constant in Territorial Communities of Settlement and Ecology, Soviet Geography, vol. XXVII: 533-53.

Gore, R. (1989): Extinction. In: Sarreth, M.E. (ed.) National Geographic Society 175 (6): 662-700.

Gould, P. (1969): Spatial Diffusion, Association of American Geographers, Resource 4: Papers 4, 6 & 19, Washington, D.C.

Griffiths, J.F. (1972): Ethiopian Highlands. In: Griffiths (ed.): World Survey of Climatology, vol.10: 369-82, New York.

Grossman, D. (1971): Do We Have a Theory of Settlement Geography? The Case of Ibo land, The Professional Geographer, vol. XXII (3): 197-203.

Grove, A.T. (1978): Africa, Third Edition, London.

Grove, A.T. (1989): The Changing Geography of Africa, Oxford University Press.

Gwadz, R.W. (1991): Malaria and Development in Africa. In: AAAS (ed.): Malaria and Development in Africa, Washington D.C: 99-103.

HABITAT (1986): Spontaneous Settlement in Rural Regions, UNCHS, Nairobi.

HABITAT (1996): The Second UNs Conference on Human Settlements, Habitat II, Istanbul.

Haining, R. (1982): Describing and Modeling Rural Settlement Maps, AAAG, vol.72 (2): 211-23.

Hansen, A. & Oliver-Smith, A. (eds) (1982): Involuntary and migration and resettlers, the problems and responses of dislocated peoples. Boulders Co., Westview Press.

Hansson, B. (1998): The question is who? The need for stakeholder analysis in a development project. In: Cederlöf, G. (ed): water the taming scarce resource. Uppsala University. Forum for Development Studies and Council for Development and Assistance Studies: 35-42.

Hawanda, T. (1989): Increasing agricultural production in Ethiopia through improved soil, water and crop management practices. Proceedings on a national workshop on food strategies for Ethiopia, Addis Ababa.

Hedberg, I. & Edward, S. (eds.) (1989): Flora of Ethiopia. (Pittosporaceae to Araliacea), vol. 3. Addis Ababa and Asmara, Ethiopia: Uppsala, Sweden.

Hill, A.R. (1987): Ecosystem Stability, Progress in Physical Geography, vol. II (3): 315-33.

Hillman, J. (1993): Ethiopia. Compendium of Wildlife Conservation Information 1, Addis Ababa.

Horvath, R. (1969): Von Thünen's Isolated State and the Area Around Addis Ababa, Ethiopia, Annals of the Association of American Geographers, vol. 59: 303-23.

Howe, G.M. (ed.) (1977): The Environment, its Influences and Hazards to Health. World Geography of Human Diseases, Academic Press, London: 3-13.

Hoyle, S.G. (1980): Nomadic Pastoral Responses to Planned Settlement. The Case of Khoshm El Girba in Eastern Sudan, Malaysian Journal of tropical Geography, vol. 2: 14-25.

Hudson, J. (1969): A Location Theory for Rural Settlement, Annals of the Association of American Geographers, vol. 59: 365-81.

Hudson, J. (1972): Geographical Diffusion Theory, Studies in Geography 19.

Hudson, F. S. (1976): Geography of Settlements, Second Edition.

Hurni, H. (1988): Land degradation, famine and land resources in Ethiopia. Pepper presented to the national conference on a disaster presentation and preparedness strategy for Ethiopia, Addis Ababa.

Hosier, R. (1988): The Ecology of Deforestation in Eastern Africa. Economic Geography, vol. 64 (2): 121-36.

Hägerstrand, T. (1965): Aspects of the Spatial Structure of Social Communication and the Diffusion of Information. Regional Science Association 16: 27-42.

Jaenson, T. (1994): The role of transecticide treated bed nets in malaria control. In: Hofvander, Y. (ed.). Nytt om U-Landshälsovård 2: 23-6.

Jahnke, H. (1983): An assessment of the recent past and present livestock situation in the Ethiopian highlands. EHRS, working paper 7, FAO, Addis Ababa.

Janssons, P. & Wery, M. (1987): Malaria in Africa South of the Sahara. Annals of Tropical Medicine and Parasitology, vol. 81 (5): 487-98.

Jansson, K., Harris, M. & Penrose, A. (1987): The Ethiopian Famine, London, Zed Books.

Johansson, S. (1992): Irrigation and Development in the Tana River Basin. In: Darkoh, M.B.K. (ed.): African River Basins and Dry land Crisies: 97-112, Uppsala.

Jones, P. (1985): Hydrology. Basil Blackwell, Oxford, England.

Jordan, T.G. (1966): On the Nature of Settlement Geography. Professional Geography, vol. 18 (1): 27.

Kaloko, F.R. (1982): Nearest-Neighbour Statistic and Settlement Pattern Analysis. Malaysian Journal of Tropical Geography, vol. 5: 13-21.

Kay, G. (1964): Aspects of Ushi Settlement History, Fort Rosebery District. In: Steel, R.W. and Prothero, M. (eds.), geographers and the tropics, London: 235-60.

King, R. (1971): The Human Factor in Agricultural Development, a Case Study from Sardinia. The Professional Geographer, vol. XXIII (3): 204-11

Kikula, I. S. (1997): Policy implications on Environment: The case of Tanzania, Stockholm.

Kleinert, H C. (1987): Settlement Pressure and the Destruction of the Forests in Rwanda (Eastern Central Africa), Applied Geography and Development, vol. 29: 93-106.

Kloos, H. (1990): Health aspects of resettlement in Ethiopia, Soc. Sci. & Med. vol. 30 (6): 643-56.

Kloos, H., Abate, T., Hailu, A. & Ayele, T. (1990): Social and ecological aspects of resettlement and Villagisation among the Konso of SW Ethiopia. Disaster, vol. 14 (4): 309-21.

Kosinski, L., Leszek, L. & Protheso, M. (eds.) (1975): People on the Move, Studies on International Migration, Methuen and Co. Lit., London.

Krafsur, E.S. (1971): Malaria Transmission in Gambela, Illubabor Province. Eth. Med. J. 2: 75-94.

Land Water Development Project (1986): Workshop on hydrology of small watersheds under H.P. hill areas, New Delhi.

Last, G.C. (1977): Patterns and problems of population resettlement in Rural Africa. In: Fassil, G. K. (ed.): introduction to rural development, IDR, Addis Ababa University, preliminary edition: 85-100.

Lealem Berhanu (1991): *Arawitochachinen Eniwok* (Lets Know Our Unique Wild Animals), *Amharic* version, Stockholm.

Learmonth, A.T.A. (1977): Malaria in world geography of human diseases. In: G.M. Howe (ed.): (Academic Press), London.

Leo Theuns, H. (1997) Reviving tourism in Sudan-political and financial constraints. Tourism recreation research 22(1): 17-25.

Leatherby, J. (1989): The millions forced to flee. In: Geographical Magazine: 14-17.

Levine, D.N. (1974): Greater Ethiopia, the evolution of a multiethnic society, Chicago.

Lewis, H.S. (1985): A Galla Monarchy. The University of Wisconsin Press, Madison.

Loevinsohn, M.E. (1994): Climatic Warming and Increased Malaria Incidence in Rwanda. LANCET, vol. 143, March 19.

Lysenko, A. J.A. & Beljaev, A.E. (1969): An Analysis of the Geographical Distribution of Plasmodium ovale. Bull. Wld. Hilth. Org. 40: 383-94.

Lösch, A. (1954): The Economics of Location, translated from the Second Revised Edition by William H. Woglom, New Haven, Yale University Press, London.

Malanson, G.P. (1985): Fire Management in Coastal Sagescrub, Southern California. Environmental Conservation vol. 12 (2):141-16.

Mannion, A. M. (1991): Global Environmental Change. John Wiley and Sons Inc., New York.

Martin, P.H., Lefebvre, M.G., Wilson, D.B., Glasgow, K.P.J. & Hocking, K.S. (1995): Malaria: Climate Sensitivity of Malaria. AMBIO, XXIV: 202-09.

May, J.M. (1961): The Ecology of Malaria. In: MAY, J. M. (ed.): Studies in Disease Ecology, New York: Chap. 8.

Mayer, W. B. (1996): Human impact on the earth, Cambridge University Press.

Myers, N. (1995): Population and biodiversity. Ambio 24 (1): 56-7.

Mbithi, P. & Barnes, C. (1975): The Spontaneous Settlements Problem in Kenya, East Africa Literature Bureau, Nirobi.

McMillan, D. (1987): The Social Impacts of Planned Settlement in Burkina Faso. In: Glantz, M. (ed.): Drought and Hunger in Africa, Cambridge, London: 297-322.

Melville, A.R., Wilson, D.B., Hocking, K.S. & Glasgow, K.J.P. (1945): Malaria in Abyssinia. East Afr. Md J. 22: 285-94.

Mengistu Woube (1986): Problems of land reform implementation in rural Ethiopia, A case study of Dejen and Wolmera districts. Geografiska Regionstudier 16. Department of Human Geography, University of Uppsala, Motala Grafiska AB.

Mengistu Woube (1987): The Geography of Hunger, Some Aspects of the Causes and Impacts of Hunger. Research Report 95, Department of Social and Economic Geography, Uppsala University, Sweden.

Mengistu Woube (1995a): Ethno botany and the Economic Role of the Selected Plant Species in Gambela. Ethiopia, Journal of Ethiopian Studies, vol. 18: 1- 26.

Mengistu Woube (1995b): Northward-southward resettlement in Ethiopia. Northeast African Studies, vol. 23 (8): 85-106.

Mengistu Woube & Sjöberg, Ö. (1995): Agrarian Reform and the Persistence of Land Fragmentation in Rural Ethiopia. African Rural and Urban Studies, vol. 1 (3):115-48

Mengistu Woube (1996): Geomorphological Studies with Special Reference to Soils in Gambela, South-Western Ethiopia. Institute of Earth Sciences, Physical Geography, Uppsala University.

Mengistu Woube (1997a): The Blue Nile river basin: the need for new conservation-based sustainability measures. SINET: Ethiop. J. Sci. 20 (1): 115-31.

Mengistu Woube (1997b): Geographical distribution and dramatic increases in incidences of malaria: consequences of the resettlement scheme in Gambela, SW Ethiopia. Indian Journal of Malariology, vol. 34 (3):140-63.

Mengistu Woube (1998): Fire Effects on Plant Communities and Soils in the Humid-Tropical Savannah of Gambela, Ethiopia. Land Degradation and Development, vol. 9 (3): 275-82.

Mengistu Woube & Sjöberg, Ö. (1999): Socialism and urbanization in Ethiopia, 1975-90. A tale of two *kebeles*. International Journal of Urban and Regional Research, vol. 23 (1): 26-44.

Mengistu Woube (1999): Floods and lack of sustainable land-water management in lower Baro-Akobo river basin, Ethiopia. Applied Geography 19 (1): 235-51.

Mengistu Woube & Sanderson, P.G. (2001): Effects of land-use on Soil Properties in the Post-Resettlement Abobo, Ethiopia. Economic Research Institute, Stockholm School of Economics and Department of Geography, Addis Ababa University. Unpublished report.

Mengistu Woube & Workneh Negatu (2002): Animal Power-Based Technological Package for Sustainable Development in Africa. Ethiopian Development Forum, vol. 1 (3): 69-93.

Merid Mekonnen (1958): Malaria Epidemic, Belessa, Begemidir Province. Unpublished field report 18, Addis Ababa.

Mesfin Wolde Mariam (1970): An Atlas of Ethiopia, Revised Edition with Additional materials, Asmara.

Mesfin Wolde Mariam (1972): An Introductory Geography of Ethiopia, Asmara.

Mesfin Wolde Mariam (1988): An assessment of stress and strain on the Ethiopian highlands. Mountain research and development, vol. 8 (4): 254-64.

Minassie Gashaw (2000): Survival strategies and ecological performances of plants in regularly burning savannah woodlands and grasslands of western Ethiopia. Gambela, Ph.D. Dissertation. Addis Ababa University, School of Graduate Studies.

Minassie Gashaw, Mekbib Eshetu Girma Mengesha, Atnaw Alefe and Geremew Tessema (2001): Preliminary survey on the wildlife resources of Gambela National Region, phase 1 study. EWCO, Unpublished report.

MoA (Ministry of Agriculture) (1988): Resettlement situation in agricultural Development, *Yekatit* 1980, E.C. (February 1988), Addis Ababa.

MoA (1989): *Begibrina Limat Yesefera Mastebaberia Tsihfet Bet, Yekatit* 1980 E.C. (Resettlement Office of the MoA), February 1988, Addis Ababa.

Ministry of Rural Development (2003): New coalition for food security in Ethiopia. Technical Group. Food Security Programme (revised), Executive Summary, October, Addis Ababa.

Moran, T.H. (1989): Adaptation and maladaptation in newly settled areas. In: D. Schuman and W. Partridge (eds). The Human ecology and tropical land settlement in Latin America. Boulder, CO, West view.

Moore, P.D. (1996): Fire damage to soils of our forests. Nature 384 (2):312-13.

Mukherji, A.B. (1976): Rural Settlements of the Chandigarh Siwalik Hills (India), a Morphogenetic Analysis, Geografiska Annaler, vol. 58 B: 95-115.

Mulongoy, K. & Merckx, R. (eds) (1993): Soil organic matter dynamics and sustainability of tropical agriculture. International Institute for tropical agriculture: Katholieke Universiteit Leuven.

Muzo, K.R. (1983): Rural Housing Improvements, Proposal on How the Church can Assist, Dar-es-Salaam.

Negussie Gebre Mariam; Abdulahi, Y. & Mebrate Assefa (1988): Malaria. In: Zein Ahmed Zein (ed.): Yellow Fever. The Ecology of Health and Diseases in Ethiopia: 136-50.

Nelson, M. (1977): Twenty-Four Resettlement Projects in Latin America, Development Digest 15: 91-103.

Norling, G. (1960): Abandonment of Rural Settlement in Väster-Botten Lappmark, North Sweden, 1930-1960. In: Geografiska Annaler, vol. 42: 232-43.

Noss, R. F. 1991. Wilderness recovery: Thinking big in restoration ecology. The environment professional 13 (3): 225.

Oba, G. (1990): Effects of Wildfire on a Semi desert Riparian Woodland along the Turkwel River, Kenya and Management Implications for Turkana Pastoralists. Land Degradation and Rehabilitation, vol. 2: 247-59.

Olsson, C. (1976): Somalias Nomader Blir Bofasta, SIDA, Stockholm

Oxby, C. (1984): Settlement Schemes for Herders in the Sub humid Tropics of West Africa, Issues of Land Rights and Ethnicity, Development Policy Review, vol. 1 (2): 217-33.

Palmer, G. (1974): The Ecology of Resettlement Schemes, Human Organization, vol. 33: 239-50.

Pankhurst, A. (1992): Resettlement and famine in Ethiopia. Manchister University Press, England.

Pankhurst, R. (1982): History of Ethiopian towns, from the middle ages to the early nineteenth century. Wiesbaden.

Parrsons, D.J. (1976): The Role of Fire in Natural Communities. Environmental Conservation vol. 3 (2): 91-100.

Perner, C. (1997): The reward of life is death, welfare and the Anyuak of the Ethiopian-Sudanese border. In: Hjort of Ornås (ed), A.Nomadic peoples: 39-54.

Phillips, J. (1975): Effects of Fire in Forest and Savannah Ecosystems of Sub-Saharan Africa. In: Kozlowski, T.T. (ed.): Fire and Ecosystems, Academic Press New York: 435-81.

Pichi-Sermolli, R. E.G. (1957): Una Carta Geobotanica Dell' Africa Orientale (Eritrea, Ethiopia, Somalia). Webbia 7:325-51.

PMAC (Provisional Military Administration Council) (1984): The Ten Year Perspective Plan (1983/84-1993-/94), Addis Ababa (in Amharic).

Pritchard, J. R. (1979): Africa, Third Edition, UK, 1979.

Prothero, R.M. (1965a): Migrants and Malaria, Longmans in Great Britain.

Prothero, R.M. (1965b): Problems of Public Health among Pastoralists, a Case Study from Africa. In: McGlashan, N.D. (ed): Medical Geography: 105-32, London.

Prothero, R.M. (1976): Disease and Mobility: A Neglected Factor in Epidemiology. African Population Mobility Project, Working Paper 26.

Ricardo, D. (1953): David Ricardo and his economics. In: Bhatta, H.L. (1994): History of Economic thought. Vikas Publishing House. Pyt LTD.

Rodgers, W.A. (1992): The conservation in East Africa. In: Bennun, L.A. (eds.): A publication of the centre for biodiversity', National Museums of Kenya: 217-30.

Ross, S.M.; Thomas, J.B. & Nortcliff, S. (1990): Soil Hydrology, Nutrient and Erosional response to the Clearance of terra Firmer Forest, Maraca Island, Roraima, Northern Brazil, Geographical Journal, vol. 136 (3): 267-82.

Rothrock, C.C. (1992): Tillage Systems and Plant Disease, Soil Science, vol. 154 (4): 308-16.

RRC (Releif and Rehabilitation Commission) (1981): Resettlement Policy, Addis Ababa.

RRC (1985): The challenges of drought, Ethiopian decade of struggle, Addis Ababa.

Salas, G. (1976): Bio element loss on clearing a tropical rainforest. Turrialba 26 (2):179-86.

Samuel, J. (1985): Ethiopian Highland Reclamation Study. Resettlement strategy, Proposals, Land-use Planning and Regulatory Department of the MoA (FAO), Working Paper 28, Addis Ababa.

Sayer, J., Caroline, H. & Mark, C.N. (eds.) (1992): Africa. The Conservation Atlas of Tropical Forests, IUCN, UK.

Scudder, T. (1973): The Human Ecology of Big Projects, River Basin Development and Resettlement. Annual Review of Anthropology 2: 45-55.

Scudder, T. (1981): The Development Potential of New Lands Resettlement in the Tropics, USAID Discussion Paper, Washington.

Shrestha, N. R. (1989): Frontiers Settlement and Landlessness among Hill Migrants in Nepal Tarai. Annals of the Association of American Geographers, vol. 9 (3): 370-89.

Sivini, G. (1986): Famine and the Resettlement Programme in Ethiopia, Unpublished Paper, University of Calabria.

Skarpe, C. (1992): Dynamics of Savannah Ecosystems. In Hytteborn, H. et al. (eds.) (1992): Vegetation Dynamics and Regeneration in Seasonal Tropical Climates. Journal of Vegetation Science 3: 293-300

Spencer, H. (1973): Tropical Pathology, Springer Verlag, Berlin.

Spensers, H.E. & Thomas, W.L. (1969): Cultural Geography as an evolutionary interest to our humanized earth (West Publishing Company, New York).

Stamp, D.L. (1964): Africa. A Study in Tropical Development, John Wiley and Sons, Inc., New York, Second Edition.

Stauder, J. (1971): The Majangir ecology and society of a southwest Ethiopian people, Cambridge Studies in Social Anthropology.

Stitz, V. (1970): The Amhara resettlement of Northern Shewa During the 18th and 19th Centuries, Rural Africana 1:70-81.

Stromgaard, P. (1988): Soil and Vegetation Changes under Shifting Cultivation in the Miombo of East Africa. Geografiska Annaler 70B (3): 363-74.

Stone, H. (1965): The Development of Focus for the Geography of Settlement. Economic Geography, vol. 41: 346-55.

Strange, L.R.N. (1980): African Pastureland Ecology. Pasture and Fodder Crop Studies 7, FAO, Rome

Taddesse Tamrat (1972): Church and state in Ethiopia, 1270-527, Oxford.

TAMS Agricultural Development Group (1976). Feasibility report: Gambela project, Phase II southwest development. United States Agency for International Development and Ministry of Agriculture of Ethiopia, Addis Ababa.

TAMS-ULG (1996): Baro-Akobo river basin Integrated Development Master Plan Project, Ministry of Water Resources, Addis Ababa.

Tayya Gebre-Mariam (Alaqa) (1922): History of the People of Ethiopia. Swedish Evangelical Mission, Asmara. Translated from the Amharic to English by Hudson, G. et al. (1987), Centre for Multiethnic Research, Uppsala.

Tesfa-Michael T-Y. (1988): Intestinal Parasitism. In: Merid Mekonnen (ed.): 195-213.

Tesfaye Awas (1996): The Ecology and Ethno botany of Indigenous Plants of Gambela Region. Master Thesis, Addis Ababa University, Department of Biology.

FDRE (The Federal Democratic Republic of Ethiopia) (1997): Environmental policy. Environmental Protection Authority in collaboration with the Ministry of Economic Development and Cooperation. Addis Ababa, April 2.

United Nations (1992): The Earth Summit (1992): Agenda 21. The UNs conference on environment and development (UNCED), 3-14 June, Rio de Janeiro, Brazil.

The Economist (1989): 27 March, London.

The New York Times (1991): Sunday, Sept. 8:13.

Thompson, I.B. (1978): Settlement and conflict in the Mediterranian World. In: the Institute of British Geographers, vol. 3 (3):255-58.

Trimingham, S. (1952): Islam in Ethiopia, Oxford University Press, London.

Tobias, P. (1978): From Linnè to Leakey Six Signposts. In: Königson, L.K (eds.); Current Argument on Early Man, published for the Royal Academy of Sciences, Pergaman Press.

Troeh, F.R., Hobbs, J.A. & Donahue, R.L. (1980): Soil and water conservation for productivity and environmental protection. Englewood Cliffs, Prentice Hall, Inc.: 25–50.

UN (1995): Integrated water resources management in Asia and the Pacific. Water Resource Series 75, New York.

UNHCR (1988): Technological Support Services in Ethiopia; Health and Nutrition Assessment of S. Sudan Refugee Camp in Keffa, Illubabor and Wello *Awrajas*: 8-22, Geneva: Annex E.

UNHCR (1991): Refugees 87, October, Geneva.

Upreti, G. (1994): Environmental conservation and sustainable development require a new development approach. Environmental Conservation, vol. 21 (1): 18-28.

USAID and MoA (1976): Feasibility Report, Gambela Project (TAMS), Phase II, SW Development.

Vavra, M. (ed.) (1995): Ecological Implications of Livestock Herbivory in the West. Department of Rangeland Ecology and Management, Texas and M University College Station.

Vidal, A. & Deraux, R.C. (1995): Evaluating forest fire hazard with a Landsat. Agricultural and Forest Meteorology 77 (3-4): 207-24.

Von Thũnen (1966): Isolated State. Edited by Hall, P. and translated by Wartemberg, C.M. London, Pergamon Press.

Walkley, A. & Black, J.A. (1934): An Examination of Degtjareff for Determining Soil Organic Matter, a Proposed Modification of the Chromic Acid Titration Method. Soil Science 34: 29-38.

Wang, L. (1986): Determination of Kjeldahl Nitrogen and Exchangeable Ammonium in Soil by the Indophenol method (NH4-N in soil extracts), Acta Agriculture Scandinavica, vol. 36 (1): 60-70.

Whelan, R.J. (1995): The Ecology of Fire, Cambridge University Press, G.B.

White, F. (1993): The Vegetation of Africa. A Descriptive memoir to accompany the UNESCO/AETFAT vegetation map of Africa. Natural Resources Research 20. UNESCO, Paris.

WHO (1992): Weekly Epidemiological Record 67:161-167, Geneva, May 29.

WHO (1994): World Malaria Situation, October-November: 3-19, Geneva.

World Commission on Environment and Development (1987): Our common future. Oxford University Press.

Whynne-Hammond, C. (1985): Elements of Human Geography, London.

Wijkman, A. & Timberlak, L. (1984): Acts of God or Acts of Man. Natural Disasters, Washington D.C. International Institute for Environment and Development.

Wolday Amha (2000): Review of microfinance development in Ethiopia: regulatory frameworks and performance. Paper presented at the symposium for reviewing Ethiopia's socioeconomic performance 1991-1999. Addis Ababa 26-9 April.

Wondatir Negatu, Beyene Petros, Mesfin Lulu, Nessibu Adugna, Robert, W. and Dejene Tilahun (1994): Some aspects of malaria prevalence, vector infectivity and DDY resistance studies in Gambela region, SW Ethiopia. Eth. J. Health Development 8 (1): 1-10.

Wood, A. (1977): A Resettlement in Illubabor province, Ethiopia, (unpublished Ph.D. Thesis), Department of Geography, University of Liverpool.

Wood, A. (1983): Population redistribution and agricultural settlement schemes in Ethiopia. In: Clark, J. I. et al. (eds.): Population and development projects in Africa. Cambridge University Press, Cambridge: 84-111.

World Bank (1991): Operational Manual, New York.

Young, A. (1976): Tropical soils and soil survey, Cambridge University Press, Cambridge.

Zein Ahmed Zein & Kloos, H. (eds.) (1988): The ecology of health and diseases in Ethiopia: 151-57, Ministry of Health, Addis Ababa.

Zewde Abate (1994): Water resource development in Ethiopia. Ithaca Press, Reading.

16 NOTES ON THE AUTHOR

Dr. Mengistu Woube is an Associate Professor in Social and Economic Geography with emphasis on natural resources, environmental and agricultural issues. He was a Visiting Scholar at Michigan State University and Visiting Research Fellow at Addis Ababa University in conjunction with a Swedish SIDA financed project in Ethiopia. Currently he has an Associate Researcher Status at the Institute of Development Research (IDR) at Addis Ababa University. Dr. Mengistu is the author of several publications on agriculture, environment, land-use, water resources, flooding, ethno botany, food security, resettlement schemes, malaria and urbanisation. He is currently working as a research consultant, and developing (i) a training programme *(Promoting Food Security through Knowledge Transfer on Food Plants* in Ethiopia) and (ii) a research project (Comparative Analysis of Irrigation Projects in Ethiopia: Techno-Institutional Regimes and Sustainable Irrigation Management for Food Security).

Printed in the United States
28837LVS00002B/3

9 781581 124835